PERSHING

★ THE | GENERALS ★

PERSHING

Commander of the Great War

★ THE | GENERALS ★

John Perry

THOMAS NELSON
Since 1798

NASHVILLE   DALLAS   MEXICO CITY   RIO DE JANEIRO

Published in Nashville, Tennessee, by Thomas Nelson. Thomas Nelson is a registered trademark of Thomas Nelson, Inc.

Published in association with the literary agency of Wolgemuth & Associates, Inc.

[If applicable, credits for photography, typesetting, or any other noteworthy vendors]

Thomas Nelson, Inc., titles may be purchased in bulk for educational, business, fund-raising, or sales promotional use. For information, please e-mail SpecialMarkets@ThomasNelson.com.

Library of Congress Cataloging-in-Publication Data
Perry, John, 1952-
Pershing : commander of the Great War / John Perry.
    p. cm. -- (The generals)
Includes bibliographical references.
ISBN 978-1-59555-355-3
1. Pershing, John J. (John Joseph), 1860-1948. 2. United States. Army--Biography. 3. Generals--United States--Biography. 4. World War, 1914-1918--United States. I. Title.
E181.P516 2011
972.08'16092--dc22
[B]
                        2011015603

Printed in the United States of America

11 12 13 14 15 WOR 6 5 4 3 2 1

To Ivy Scarborough, whose patriotism, strength of character, devotion to duty, and compassion for others make him a man of honor in the Pershing mold, and whose kindness, generosity, and encouragement make him a precious friend.

Contents

A Note from the Editor

To CONTEMPLATE THE lives of America's generals is to behold both the best of us as a nation and the lesser angels of human nature, to bask in genius and to be repulsed by arrogance and folly. It is these dichotomies that have defined the widely differing attitudes toward the "man on horseback," which have alternatively shaped the eras of our national memory. We have had our seasons of hagiography, in which our commanders can do no wrong and in which they are presented to the young, in particular, as unerring examples of nobility and manhood. We have had our revisionist seasons, in which all power corrupts—military power in particular—and in which the general is a reviled symbol of societal ills.

Fortunately, we have matured. We have left our adolescence

with its gushing extremes and have come to a more temperate view. Now, we are capable as a nation of celebrating Washington's gifts to us while admitting that he was not always a gifted tactician in the field. We can honor Patton's battlefield genius and decry the deformities of soul that diminished him. We can learn both from MacArthur at Inchon and from MacArthur at Wake Island.

We can also move beyond the mythologies of film and leaden textbook to know the vital humanity and the agonizing conflicts, to find a literary experience of war that puts the smell of boot leather and canvas in the nostrils and both the horror and the glory of battle in the heart. This will endear our nation's generals to us and help us learn the lessons they have to teach. Of this we are in desperate need, for they offer lessons of manhood in an age of androgyny, of courage in an age of terror, of prescience in an age of myopia, and of self-mastery in an age of sloth. To know their story and their meaning, then, is the goal here, in the hope that we will emerge from the experience a more learned, perhaps more gallant, and, certainly, more grateful people.

Stephen Mansfield

Series Editor, *The Generals*

Introduction

NO OTHER AMERICAN military leader is as important and yet as little known as John J. Pershing. He led an army of more than a million men in France, defeating the seemingly invincible German war machine after only six months of offensive action. Russia had crumbled into anarchy; Britain and France had fallen on their knees after three years of horrific fighting. Pershing crossed the Atlantic determined to do battle a different way. To carry out his plan, he had to fight a political war with his allies. They insisted on continuing as before. Seeing the failure of their approach, Pershing refused.

When the French general-in-chief relieved him of command, Pershing ignored the order and went on to stop the Germans forty-five miles from Paris, saving a nation and probably a continent. By the time he sailed home, Pershing had become the only U.S. army officer in history to be commissioned General of the Armies during his lifetime. The one other soldier so honored, a century and a half after his death, was George Washington.

It was Pershing, more than anyone else, who brought the American army into the modern era. He saw the power of twentieth-century weapons for the first time as an observer during the Russo-Japanese War. The machine gun and other innovations used in that war changed warfare forever. Pershing was a keen observer, a lifelong student and teacher. What he learned in Manchuria, he taught in Mexico more than a decade later when President Wilson sent him to retaliate against Pancho Villa. For the first time, American divisions fought using radios and air support. During World War I, Pershing and his tactical genius aide, George C. Marshall, executed the first battle in American history to coordinate infantry, artillery, tanks, and air support. Troops were armed with machine guns, hand grenades, and poison gas. Draft horses shared the miserable roads with motorized trucks and the general's limousine, the latter fitted with double rear wheels to negotiate the mud.

Pershing returned to the United States a hero. There was a ticker tape parade in New York, an address to a joint session of Congress, rumors of a presidential bid, gossip about the society women the handsome widower was dating, and a Pulitzer Prize for his history of "the war to end all war."

And yet today General Pershing has faded away to the second or third tier of America's historical consciousness. While some of us have heard the name, many more have not. His accomplishments rightly place him in the company of great generals such as MacArthur, Eisenhower, and Patton, all of whom he commanded and inspired, and all of whom he outranked. He shaped world events in Europe as surely as Woodrow Wilson or David Lloyd George. Had they listened to him about forcing Germany into unconditional surrender, his influence would have been even greater. He served with Theodore Roosevelt in Cuba—Pershing was at San Juan Hill—and headed the American Expeditionary Force when one of its junior officers was a captain from Missouri named Harry Truman. Still, for all that, Pershing's light has dimmed with time while Roosevelt's and Truman's have not.

Part of the reason—a large part, some would claim—is that, as a public figure, John J. Pershing was not a lovable man. Roosevelt (both of them), Truman, Churchill, de Gaulle, and other contemporaries were seen as compassionate, dedicated, inspiring, and personable figures. Yes, FDR was elitist, Truman coarse with his language, de Gaulle conceited (he once declared, "I am France"), and all great men have their shortcomings. But these were people the public would gladly invite to dinner.

To most of the millions of men he commanded during his career, John J. Pershing was not likable in the least. He was instead an insufferable nitpicker obsessed with the smallest detail of military regimentation. Troops dreaded the sight of the massive limousine flying the four-star general's flag. Its arrival meant a long list of deficiencies in need of correcting immediately: dirty kitchen pots, untidy garbage dumps, scuffed boots, soiled uniforms, sloppy marching. Nothing imperfect escaped his notice or criticism. With war raging all around, he would send word to battalion commanders to make sure their men shaved every day.

Pershing got the first iteration of his nickname from angry West Point cadets. In a place where extreme regimentation was the order of the day, Pershing was despised for his over-the-top enforcement of the smallest rule. Knowing that his first command had been black cavalry troops on the frontier, his students christened him "Nigger Jack." Newspaper writers later softened it to "Black Jack."

What none of his students and only a handful of professional colleagues ever saw was the other John J. Pershing, the one who was a wonderful dancer, tender husband, faithful friend, reliable confidant, and devoted father. His love letters to his wife and his conversations with close friends after her death reveal a man who felt his emotions deeply and who acknowledged and understood them as few men ever do. He enjoyed whiskey and, as a single man, the company of women. He quit playing poker because he was so good at it he thought it might become an obsession. He loved innocent jokes and high jinks, late nights and good wine. He kept this life completely separate from his professional one. No friendship or pastime ever got in the way of absolute fidelity to his duty. To that small group fortunate enough to know the poker-playing dancer, Pershing was a great and wonderful man. To the rest, he was stiff—cold, impersonal, and best avoided.

Pershing was the way he was because he knew that winning wars was in the details. Troops who paid attention to the small things would master the big things. He learned from his experiences in Cuba and the Philippines that no matter how well trained or dedicated a soldier was, victory in battle might well depend on clean drinking water, well-shod artillery horses, and efficient stevedores at the dock. What he learned, he taught, marshalling his resources and preparing his men in France until King George himself complained to President Wilson that the American general wasn't willing to fight. Pershing held his ground and then accomplished in a few months what George and his army hadn't done in years.

In addition to having a cold, unattractive public image, Pershing absolutely did not care what his image was. The fact that history has shortchanged him would not have mattered to him in the least. Most great figures spend time grooming their public image. General Pershing did the opposite. He accepted most of the accolades showered upon him after the war but did nothing to shape his own legacy. He despised writing his history of the war, which took years and produced an amazingly boring narrative more than eight hundred pages long. The general knew it was dull but thought it was his duty to tell the story as accurately and fairly as possible. When he heard he was being considered for the Medal of Honor, Pershing took steps to stop the process. He had only done his duty, he declared, and that included leading his men from the front.

The real General Pershing was a great man who combined the brave, patriotic, innovative, dedicated persona of the leader of the American Expeditionary Force with the compassionate, tender, loving, gentle, forgiving human being so few people ever knew. An effective leader has to be hard and strong, inflexible and impermeable. Pershing accepted this as the responsibility of leadership. The role of husband, father, and friend was different. John J. Pershing excelled in all arenas. And the closer we look, the more clearly we see how each side of his humanity inspired the other.

Soli Deo Gloria

John Perry

Nashville, Tennessee

New Year's Day 2011

ONE

Teacher and Student

JOHN JOSEPH PERSHING'S first memories were of war. He was a few months shy of his fourth birthday when on June 18, 1864, Captain Clifton Holtzclaw led a Confederate raid on his hometown of Laclede, Missouri. John Fletcher Pershing and his wife, Anne Elizabeth, had raised little Jackie in a home loyal to the Union. Though Missouri remained officially part of the United States, its citizens were sharply divided. Only President Lincoln's intervention with federal troops had kept the state from splitting the way Virginia had, where Union sympathizers left the Confederacy to form West Virginia. As it was, Missouri was an unsettled, lawless, often dangerous place. In practical terms it stood neither solidly Union nor Confederate. It was a slaveholding Northern state where brother fought against brother, raiders and profiteers from both sides roamed at large, and a town might be occupied by Bluecoats one day and Rebels the next.

Laclede was a small farming community in north central Missouri, away from the worst of the intense fighting in the South and in the southwest part of the state. Yet loyalties ran deep and tempers flared in the opening months of the war as neighbors took their stands for one side or the other. John and Anne boldly displayed their loyalty to the Union by raising the Stars and Stripes over their house. Confederate supporters in town said if John didn't take the flag down, they'd do it for him. After he promised to shoot anybody who tried, they changed their minds and left the flag alone.

John Pershing ran the general store in Laclede and also supplied the local Union soldiers, two regiments of Missouri Volunteers, with everything from spurs to toothbrushes. For this reason and because of the flag incident, Pershing was a prime target of the ragtag unofficial raiding party that galloped into town that June afternoon. As invaders charged in through the front door of the store, Pershing ran out the back. The raiders went to Pershing's house where Jackie, his mother, and his infant brother, Jim, waited in terror. After the invaders searched the rooms and left, John came in the back door with a shotgun, determined to fight. Jackie's mother screamed at him to lie flat on the floor. He watched as she put her arms around his father and begged him not to fight, for her sake and the boys'. If he fired, she knew he would be killed and maybe the rest of them as well. Pershing put his gun down and waited for the marauders to finish their work and leave. They ransacked his store, stealing all the merchandise they could carry and three thousand dollars in cash.

In the wake of the attack, men in the community formed a home guard, electing Pershing lieutenant and later captain, but there were no more raids. In less than a year the war was over. By then Jackie was a familiar figure at the Missouri Volunteers commissary, where he sometimes went with his father on business. The supply sergeant gave the boy hardtack "rations" that he carried home with pride. Seeing how he liked playing soldier, his mother made him a child-sized uniform for his "marches" to camp and back.

Even after the war ended, Laclede remained an unpredictable and sometimes wild place. Veterans from both sides drifted in and out, and homesteaders heading west passed through on their way to a new life on the frontier. John Pershing prospered, adding a lumberyard and other businesses to his thriving store trade. Within a few years he was the richest man in the county and moved his family into a fine two-story house inside a trim white picket fence. In time Jackie and Jim had seven more brothers and sisters. The Pershings helped start a new Methodist church in town and held its quarterly business meetings in their home. Jackie, also called Jack or Johnny as he grew older, went to school, ran barefoot in summers except for Sundays, attended church, and got in his share of trouble for stealing peaches, fighting, and harassing neighborhood animals.

He was old enough to read about the Franco-Prussian War in the St. Louis newspapers in 1870, though by that time his early fascination with soldiering had faded. Johnny decided he wanted to be a lawyer. He went with his father to see his attorney at the Linn County seat of Linneus, watched him represent Pershing's business interests in court, and said he would go to law school some day. For the time being, he had his hands full with farm chores and school. His father invested heavily in real estate, buying two farms and large tracts of timber. Besides the usual chores of milking, chopping firewood, feeding the animals, and repairing equipment, Johnny learned to break horses, plow, and drive the huge reaper at harvest time. As he worked, he daydreamed of college and law school at the University of Missouri.

What neither Johnny nor anyone else could have imagined was that a settlement at the end of the war he'd read about set off a chain of events that financially ruined the Pershing family. A coalition of German states defeated France under Napoleon III, nephew of the great general and emperor. One of the spoils of victory was a large payment in gold, which prompted the German confederation to stop minting silver coins. Much of the world's silver was mined in the United States, so this decision caused a steep drop in the domestic silver market. In 1873 the United States, which had backed its paper money with both silver and gold, decided to move to a gold-only system as well. This policy led to high interest rates—a special burden to farmers and small businessmen—and a loss of confidence in financial markets, which were already overextended by heavy investment in a nationwide railroad expansion. Eighteen thousand banks and businesses failed within two years, driving unemployment to 14 percent.

These events rearranged Johnny's future. College was

suddenly out of the question. His father lost his store and almost all his land to foreclosure, hanging on to the fine white house in town and one heavily mortgaged farm of 160 acres. John Pershing went on the road as a traveling salesman and his wife took in boarders. Johnny and Jim, thirteen and eleven, were put in charge of the farm, responsible for raising food and earning money to help the family along as best they could. Johnny had to quit school, except for a few weeks in the winter when it was too cold to go into the fields.

The brothers held on bravely for three years through drought, depressed prices, and an invasion of grasshoppers, until that farm, too, was foreclosed. Johnny still dreamed of being a lawyer but knew that for now he had to contribute to the household income. At seventeen he took a job teaching at a school for black children, despite his own lack of education. His father had once been the richest man in town; now young John was taunted by his peers for teaching the children of former slaves. Seeing him on his way to class, they called out, "Nigger!"

The jeers didn't deter him. He kept the job a year, reading law books on his own as time allowed. Before he was twenty he had read all the works of William Blackstone, the British lawyer and judge whose principles helped shape the U.S. Constitution. In 1879 he received a one-year appointment to teach at a white school ten miles away in Prairie Mound. The pay was forty dollars a month, ten of which went for room and board. The youngest of his forty-five pupils was six and the oldest twenty-one. Teaching there gave John Pershing some of the first lessons in leadership that would one day play such an important role in shaping his character. The oldest student, two years older than Pershing, once bullied another student. As punishment Pershing told him he had to stay after school. Yet when class was over, he got up to leave with everyone else. Pershing flew off the platform at the front of the room where he stood to teach and planted himself inches from the student.

"I am here to run this school," he declared. "You will obey me or you will face the consequences," meaning a whipping with the switch that stood ever ready in the corner. The student backed down. Pershing accepted his responsibility to uphold the school standards and to make someone under him toe the line. The boy was bigger than he was, and the school board would probably have taken up such a discipline problem instead of forcing a young, inexperienced teacher to deal with it. None of that mattered. Pershing was in charge; he was responsible. Rules were rules; he'd given an order, and that was the end of it.

Another time a student's enraged father came to school with a shotgun. Pershing met him outside and challenged him to get off his horse, put down his gun, and the two of them would fight it out. They fought and Pershing won. Then he dressed the father's cuts. Again Pershing was in charge, saw his duty, and carried it out regardless of the circumstances.

To get to law school Pershing had to earn more money. To do that he had to get a better position, which meant earning a degree from a teacher's college. He spent the summer at the state teacher's school in Kirksville, then taught a second year in Prairie Mound, followed by another summer of schooling, and a third year teaching in 1881.

The summer of 1881, Pershing was back in Kirksville again, where his sister Elizabeth had also enrolled. Reading the newspaper one Saturday, he saw that there would be an exam to select a student from their congressional district for an appointment to the U.S. Military Academy at West Point, New York. He and Elizabeth, called Beth, talked about it. John had never considered a military career and didn't know much about the Academy except that great Civil War generals had gone there, including the senior commanders from both sides, Ulysses S. Grant and Robert E. Lee. That connection appealed to him, as did the fact that tuition was free to everyone who was admitted. He could get through college much faster if he didn't have to teach most of the year to pay for a few months of summer courses. Academy graduates also had guaranteed jobs as commissioned officers. The military commission meant less to him than the fact that a West Point education would make him a better teacher and, one day, a better lawyer. He imagined himself a leader in the lecture hall or the courtroom, not on the battlefield.

John's sister encouraged him to apply and helped him study for the local admissions tests. Eighteen candidates gathered in Trenton, Missouri, to compete for the honor of applying to West Point from their district. Through a battery of written and oral exams, students were eliminated until only two were left. The examiner asked the other applicant to explain the function of the infinitive in the sentence "I love to study." He got it wrong. Then it was John Pershing's turn. He correctly answered that the infinitive "to study" is the object of the verb.

When his mother heard that John had won the competition

and would take the admissions test at West Point, she was proud of her son. Until then she hadn't realized, though, that graduates from the Academy had to serve in the army. When she heard the truth, it made her anxious to think her firstborn would be traveling out of state for the first time in his life to go to college and then become a lieutenant in the army. It would have eased her motherly burden if, like her son and most of the rest of the country, she had believed American soldiers would not go to war again in the foreseeable future. What was there to fight about? The country had knit itself back together after the Civil War, its boundaries stretched from coast to coast, and its borders with Mexico on the south and British Canada on the north were peaceful and secure. Oceans separated it from other foreign powers to the east and west. About the only fighting on the horizon was against Indians as settlers continued pouring westward and crowding them off their traditional homelands. Still, Mrs. Pershing sensed looming war and worried.

Like a number of other West Point applicants, Pershing went to New York months ahead of the entrance exam to enroll in a prep school that specialized in Academy admissions tests. The course at Colonel Huse's School in Highland Falls was four months long and carefully tailored to the military curriculum. Since the school was just outside the entrance gate, Pershing and his eleven Huse classmates could go onto the Academy grounds for the evening parade and retiring of the colors. As he watched, it seemed almost impossible that he might soon be one of those cadets in their immaculate uniforms marching with absolute precision.

That year, all twelve of Colonel Huse's hopefuls passed their tests to join the class of 1886. Cadet Pershing began the summer ahead of his first, or plebe, academic year, with the other 128 members of his class in "Beast Barracks." Before the Civil War, a cadet's first West Point experience was summer camp—living in tents, marching long hours, and enduring punishing drills and exercises to equip him physically and mentally for life at the Academy. After the war, in order to prepare even more fully for what lay ahead, the cadets spent three weeks before summer camp segregated in the barracks under the command of upperclassmen. These intense weeks were designed to break down the individual cadet and remake him as part of a cohesive military unit. Students were treated like wild beasts being broken, hence the name Beast Barracks.

The "Beast" experience taught a cadet to obey immediately and without question, to think under pressure, to control the onset of panic, and to go beyond what he thought was the limit of his endurance—all essential characteristics of a military leader. Cadet Pershing quickly realized that grammar, geography, history, and everything he'd studied for his entrance exam meant nothing for now. What was important was following orders instantly, completely, and with enthusiasm. Duty and discipline were the only standard.

New cadets were at the mercy of their upperclassmen superiors. Upperclassmen yelled at them for everything, criticized them mercilessly, and punished them incessantly. Plebes had to stand at an exaggerated form of attention with their chins on their chests and shoulders square. Their clothing had to be in order and spotless at all times. They could never be late for anything, never question an order, never talk back. They spent hours practicing the most basic marching drills, learning the fine points of military courtesy and decorum, and keeping their quarters and the campus immaculate.

Exhausted after a grueling day of marching, they could be awakened in the middle of the night for foot inspection or any other whim of the upperclassmen. For the least mistake, an upperclassman could order a plebe to do almost anything: chew on rope, eat soap, pick up all the ants in an anthill one at a time, eat with his feet off the floor, balance on his stomach on a pole and pretend to swim, do deep knee bends until he passed out, stand at attention on his head, or whatever else he could think of.

After the rigors of Beast Barracks and summer camp, the plebes moved into their dormitories to start the fall term, though the intense hazing continued relentlessly.

The Academy curriculum covered all the traditional academic subjects including English, mathematics, history, chemistry, and French. Then there were military subjects from fencing and riding to gunnery and tactics, plus endless hours of marching, drill, inspection, and parades. These last were heavily emphasized, and cadets received demerits for the slightest infraction. A crooked cap, a muddy boot, talking or moving in ranks, excessive arm swinging while walking, or any one of a hundred other tiny mistakes drew a tongue lashing and a demerit, known informally as a "skin."

The summer Pershing enrolled at West Point, the superintendent was General Oliver Otis Howard, a devout Christian who had lost his right arm during the Civil War and later received the Medal of Honor. Otis had previously headed the Freedman's Bureau, formed to assimilate freed slaves into American society, and he helped found a college for them in Washington DC that was named Howard University in his honor. In 1882 Howard left West Point to command the army in the western plains. His replacement was Colonel Wesley Merritt, also a Civil War veteran, who served under General George Armstrong Custer before leading troops in Texas and on the western frontier. The latest in a long line of notorious disciplinarians, Merritt was considered the most rigid and inflexible of all. Of the 129 plebes who reported to Beast Barracks in the spring of 1882, only seventy-seven survived to graduate in 1886.

As a cadet Pershing developed the two sides of his personality that would shape his philosophy as a military leader. As an individual and as a friend, Pershing was warm, cordial, fun-loving, adventurous, and willing to risk punishment for the chance to enjoy himself. He earned more than two hundred skins during his West Point years, many of them for studying after hours and other time-related infractions, while twenty of his classmates got none at all. Pershing loved drinking and merrymaking and had a keen eye for the ladies, regularly escorting them along Flirtation Walk on campus, where tradition held that a girl could not refuse a cadet's request for a kiss. Trim and handsome at six feet and 180 pounds, Pershing was very popular with the opposite sex.

When it came to military matters and responsibilities of command, however, Cadet Pershing was all business. He developed a ramrod straight posture and bearing, a concise, commanding manner of speech, a hatred of sloppiness or laziness, and an unwavering adherence to rules and regulations. As an upper-classman he was at least as relentless as older cadets had once been with him—probably more so—when it came to a scrap of paper on the ground, a smudge on a boot, or a water spot on a washstand. Rules were to be obeyed instantly and completely. Another aspect of Pershing's developing personality was that in exercising military command, nothing he said or demanded was on a personal level. His orders and expectations were imper-sonal, inflexible, dispassionate, and by the book. Underclassmen who would have personally resented another cadet for the same treatment did not resent Pershing because there was no tinge of personal criticism. What he demanded was simply a matter of fol-lowing orders. Friendships and personalities were not a factor.

As his graduation approached, Cadet Pershing still planned to serve out his military commitment and then go to law school. Yet despite his evident lack of interest in a long-term military career, his peers regarded him as a leader. Though he would grad-uate only thirtieth in his class, Pershing was elected first captain for his senior year, the highest student honor in the school. His election was announced at the graduation ceremonies in 1885, marking the move of the class of '86 into the first-year, or senior, position. Long afterward Pershing recalled that he had his new rank insignia on his sleeve within five minutes. "No other mili-tary promotion has ever come to me quite equal to that," he said. It was one of the proudest moments of his life.[1]

Newly appointed first captain in the summer of 1885, Pershing commanded an honor guard trackside as the funeral train of former president and general Ulysses S. Grant went past. He enjoyed the opportunity to salute General William T. Sherman, Civil War hero and Academy graduate, on his frequent visits to campus. He also had the pleasure of entertaining Mark Twain in his room, where the renowned author and humorist spun an evening of yarns for his barracks mates, referring to Pershing as his "fellow Missourian."

After graduating from the Academy on June 11, 1886, Pershing and some classmates took the ferry fifty miles down the Hudson to New York City, where they spent a couple of days and nights in the city. There were celebration banquets at Martinelli's and Delmonico's, where the spirits flowed freely. Nursing hangovers, the men toured the newly completed Brooklyn Bridge, visited department stores and a wax museum, and rode the elevated train. Once the party ended, Pershing, freshly commissioned a second lieutenant, went home to Laclede for the summer. In September he traveled back east to Washington DC to receive his first duty assignment; he then rode the train west with the other members of the class of '86 who were stationed out that direction. "A jollier crowd than ours never traveled," Pershing later recalled. "We told stories, sang class songs, cleaned out eating houses, fired at prairie dogs, hazed the peanut boy, and practically ran the train."[2]

The lieutenants got off at their various duty stations along the way. Pershing found himself in an alien land of "burro, cactus, and tarantula"[3] in the New Mexico desert. Fort Bayard was a dusty, desolate frontier outpost of the Sixth Cavalry and Second Lieutenant John J. Pershing's new home.

Cadet Pershing in 1886, the year he graduated from West Point and received his commission. He had not planned on a military career but wanted a good education to prepare him for teaching and law.

Captain Pershing (under umbrella) with a Moro Filipino interpreter, Iligan, c. 1902. Pershing took time to learn Moro customs in order to encourage negotiation and limit conflict.

Days after Helen Frances Warren met Captain Pershing she wrote, "Have lost my heart." Twenty years younger than the captain, "Frankie" was the daughter of Senator Francis Warren, the richest man in Wyoming. The Pershings were married in 1905.

General and Mrs. Pershing and three of their children, Helen, Anne, and Warren in the Philippines c. 1911. Their fourth child, Mary, was born in 1912.

T W O

High Words of Praise

THE U.S. ARMY was a very minor operation in the 1880s. More than three million soldiers had fought in the Civil War on both sides; between six and seven hundred thousand lost their lives. More men died on the battlefield during May 1864 than the total number of men in uniform twenty years later. Lieutenant Pershing was then one of two thousand American officers leading about twenty-five thousand enlisted men of all arms. Except for isolated installations like Fort Bayard and engineering projects such as building harbors, bridges, and dams, about the only work for soldiers was among diplomatic and political circles in the East. There, duties consisted largely of consular service, attending meetings and receptions, and handing out engraved calling cards.

Fort Bayard was a settlement of about three hundred built in

a quadrangle around a central parade ground, scratched out of
the barren New Mexico desert 150 miles northwest of El Paso,
Texas. For the soldiers, most days were a boring combination of
maintenance and drill—riding, jumping, target practice, saber
lessons—with patrols into the surrounding desert that seldom
encountered anything but snakes and scorpions. Lieutenant
Pershing's first assignment was to build a chain of heliograph
stations between Fort Bayard and another Sixth Cavalry post at
Fort Stanton. These installations, on hilltops twenty-five or thirty
miles apart, consisted of huge mirrors that signalmen used to
flash Morse code messages back and forth along the peaks for
communication between the forts.

In October 1886, his second month in New Mexico, Pershing
began searching for a renegade band of Apaches rumored to be
raiding white settlers. Assembling with other cavalrymen to begin
their patrol, Pershing was shocked to find the soldiers drunk. In
camp the first night out, their horses were spooked and ran off.
This was not the kind of performance his years at West Point had
prepared him for. The natives soon turned themselves in, which
was doubtless a relief to the lieutenant under the circumstances.

Pershing settled into his role as a junior officer, commanding enlisted men far older than himself in patrolling the desert,
building roads, putting up buildings, and capturing thieves and
deserters. Officers and enlisted ranks lived very different lives
in the Sixth Cavalry, as they did elsewhere in the service. While
the sergeants and their subordinates shouldered the heavy lifting
around the fort, officers upheld Eastern traditions of social for-
mality as though they were still in Washington or New York. They

paid formal calls on each other in full dress uniform, their wives dined with them in evening gowns, and everyone ate off fine china and silver brought by rail and wagon into the middle of nowhere a hundred miles from the nearest post office.

Pershing came to love the vast, quiet majesty of the desert. Though a novice at gambling, he quickly became so good at poker that he stopped playing because he considered it too much of a distraction. Two of Pershing's best friends were Lieutenants Richard Paddock and Julius Penn, the latter also a classmate. The three green officers, who lived together, were soon known around the fort as the "Green Ps." The trio shared a Chinese cook. "We are living like kings," Pershing wrote to a friend, listing the bumper crop of vegetables along with milk, quail, turkey, and other delights that the cook prepared daily for the Green Ps.[1] Pershing loved to fish and found places to cast a line even in the desert— Silver City, along the San Francisco River, was nine miles away. On one trip he and his friends caught 240 trout. There was abundant feed for the animals and plenty of good water and firewood. All the lieutenant missed, he admitted to his friend Lieutenant Penn, was female companionship.

Pershing had already established the lifelong habit of being fun-loving and friendly on one hand but a stickler for rules and decorum when in command. Now other character traits revealed themselves that would serve him well. Pershing was patient and compassionate toward people of other cultures, even when public opinion tended toward the opposite. At this point in history, Native Americans in general were derided as savages. They were portrayed as half-animals who attacked innocent settlers, pagan, naked, ignorant, prone to violence and alcoholism, a threat to decent people and a blight on the earth. Pershing decided that rather than hunting them down, a better way to deal with Indians was to get to know them, understand their fears and needs, gain their trust, and find a peaceful means of settling the white man's differences with them. To the lieutenant, fighting was a last resort, only after all talk and negotiation had failed.

Pershing invited discussion with Indians, listened to their stories, and watched their dances. Once he saw a brave stalking a deer while wearing antlers on his head and imagined a native legend come to life. He sat with tribesmen around their bonfires and shared their meal of boiled dog. The natives' trust in Pershing allowed him to negotiate rather than fight, avoiding bloodshed under circumstances that typically led to injury and death on both sides and deeper distrust between them.

In one case Pershing and a patrol went to the aid of two settlers barricaded in a log cabin against a hundred Indians. Rather than attacking, Pershing negotiated with the chiefs, ending the standoff without a shot being fired. A more complicated challenge was rescuing white cattle thieves who had killed a Zuñi while trying to steal his herd. They were now under attack, along with some innocent cowboys the natives assumed were in on the scheme. Through patient diplomacy, Pershing rescued the cowboys and took custody of the robbers, again without firing a shot.

In both instances, Pershing made it clear that he would prevail no matter what. Force was always an option, but he would not risk his men's safety as long as there was an alternate solution. His native friends once asked Pershing if he would wrestle their top competitor. Determined to be honest with them in all things, he said he would not because the native was too dirty. They challenged him to a footrace instead, which he accepted. With a crowd of Indians and soldiers looking on, the lieutenant and the brave sped off. Betting on both sides was heavy. With only a few strides to go, Pershing's ankle buckled. As he fell, he rolled over the finish line the winner. In honor of his victory, his hosts awarded him a new name: Man Who Crawls to Win. Pershing would not allow his soldiers to collect on their bets. He was convinced that Indians had suffered enough at the hands of the government. Their low state, he believed, was "mainly the result of government neglect and insincerity" that produced "the most cruel, unjust, blackest page of American history."[2]

His compassion toward Native Americans did not protect him from danger. On patrol one day he was knocked off his horse by an Apache who then prepared either to scalp or kill him with his tomahawk. At the last instant the attacker was distracted by the sight of Pershing's army revolver, stole it, and then rode away, leaving the lieutenant in the dirt, bruised but safe.

Lieutenant Pershing served at Forts Bayard and Stanton before being assigned to Fort Wingate, sixteen miles from Gallup, New Mexico. Though he had come to love the desert, he had nothing nice to say about his new post. To a friend back at Stanton, he wrote, "I have been there so long and had so much fun and know so many people, that I hated to leave. This post is [nothing but] . . . tumble down old quarters, the winters are severe, it is always bleak and the surrounding country is barren."[3]

In June 1887 Pershing and another lieutenant from Fort

Wingate, John Stotsenburg, left on a two-hundred-mile trip to the Grand Canyon. They had two pack mules loaded with supplies, a cook–animal handler–helper named Minus, and a Navajo scout named Sam. They visited Indian settlements along the way and also a small community of Mormon settlers. All seemed well until Sam's horse developed a problem and Sam left the group to get another one. After a long wait, the officers realized their guide was gone for good, meaning they would have to find the trail on their own. They got lost and began running low on water. The animals turned finicky—when one of the horses kicked Lieutenant Pershing he kicked it back—and the three travelers began rationing what water they had, softening their breakfast biscuits with whiskey to save every drop. Coming upon a stream, they filled their canteens and then filled the coffee pot, stuffing the spout with grass so as not to spill even a little.

During the night Minus panicked and deserted the camp, taking the mules with him. The two lieutenants threw away everything they could do without, including their weapons. They struggled on, finally making contact with their long-lost Navajo guide, who had water for them. As they rested Minus appeared, crazed with thirst and filthy from eating mud. Welcomed at a desolate cabin, they feasted on antelope steaks and, at last, gazed down at the Grand Canyon. Once they made it back to Fort Wingate, Lieutenant Stotsenburg declared they were perfectly satisfied that they knew now how *not* to go to the Grand Canyon.

In the winter of 1890–91, Lieutenant Pershing served on the fringes of what would be the last major battle between the army and native tribes. A Paiute medicine man saw a vision of Christ returning to earth, reviving dead tribal members, replenishing the herds of buffalo decimated by white hunters, and bringing paradise to all who were displaced by whites and hunted by the cavalry. The Indian Death Song would be replaced by the Ghost Dance celebrating the return of deceased loved ones and lost riches. Rumors spread that Sitting Bull, the famous Lakota Sioux chief and shaman who had predicted Custer's defeat at Little Big Horn, was inspired by this vision to take his followers on the warpath.

On November 23, Pershing and the Sixth took the train to Rapid City, South Dakota, to defend against a possible attack. There they were issued buffalo coats and muskrat caps against the bitter cold. Native Americans working as police for the federal government went to arrest Sitting Bull on December 15. The chief's supporters resisted and opened fire. The policemen shot back, killing Sitting Bull with a bullet to the head and another in the side. That same day orders went out for the Sixth to capture another Lakota Sioux leader, the Minniconjou chief Big Foot. But on December 29, Big Foot turned himself and his tribe in at the Pine Ridge Indian Reservation. Women and children traveling with him needed protection from the severe weather. The Seventh Cavalry, Custer's old unit, was on duty at Pine Ridge and demanded the Indians hand over their guns.

Someone fired a shot. The soldiers opened fire indiscriminately with rifles and cannon, slaughtering natives and each other along Wounded Knee Creek. Big Foot was one of the first to die. He was later found frozen half upright, as though he had being trying to struggle to his feet at the moment of death. Sioux women with children in their arms were shot down as they ran. Eyewitnesses reported women carrying babies being chased as far as two miles before being caught and killed; Indian boys coming out of hiding only to be butchered with cavalry sabers; an infant still nursing at its dead mother's breast. More than a hundred native men, women, and children died; some reports put the figure as high as three hundred. About fifty American soldiers also fell, most of them killed by their fellow soldiers.

A court of inquiry exonerated the commander of the Seventh Cavalry, Colonel James W. Forsyth, though his commanding general, Nelson A. Miles, was appalled and outraged by what had happened. Most of the public had no idea what actually took place. They clung to the myth of Indians as murderous savages. A young reporter named Frank L. Baum, who would later gain international fame for his *Wizard of Oz* stories, spoke for many when he wrote of the Wounded Knee massacre:

> Our only safety depends upon the total extermination of the Indians. Having wronged them for centuries, we had better, in order to protect our civilization, follow it up by one more wrong and wipe these untamed and untamable creatures from the face of the earth. In this lies future safety for our settlers and the soldiers who are under incompetent commands. Otherwise, we may expect future years to be as full of trouble with the redskins as those have been in the past.[4]

If Lieutenant Pershing had any opinion on the deaths of Big Foot and his followers, he kept it to himself. He had duties to perform. He was assigned to lead a troop of Oglala scouts patrolling Pine Ridge, including the site of the massacre, where bodies still lay frozen on the ground. He began teaching them scouting techniques but soon realized it was all second nature to them and they were already experts. He quickly earned their trust and respect. When they came across Sioux looking for relatives among the dead, the scouts made themselves Pershing's bodyguards, keeping close watch in case a native, seeing a white soldier, suddenly had thoughts of revenge.

To close this tragic chapter in the relationship between the government and the Indians on a brighter note, and to demonstrate the invincible firepower of the United States, General Miles ordered a huge military parade and invited ten thousand Sioux to watch. Pershing was there, as were several of his West Point classmates. The cavalry marched, along with the bugle corps, hospital and supply wagons, artillery guns mounted on their caissons, companies of infantry, and the African American "Buffalo Soldiers" of the Ninth Cavalry.

Pershing enjoyed the festivities immensely, wryly admitting that he stuffed himself to excess with food and drink and that it wasn't the first time he had done so. To a friend he wrote, "Three or four of the boys got a little too full, one of whom I am which. I never went to a reunion yet that I did not wind up full as eighteen goats."[5] Here Pershing revealed a glimpse of the hearty merrymaker few people outside his inner circle ever saw.

The Indian wars were over for good. Pershing was reassigned to the University of Nebraska at Lincoln, where his new post was professor of military science and tactics and commandant of cadets. Commanding troops and teaching students had a lot in common. Pershing's experience as an officer enhanced his skills and reaffirmed his interest as an educator. Now he would combine the roles of commander and teacher, further refining leadership characteristics that were already apparent in his life: fairness, a sense of duty, jovial friendship in the off hours, and unflinching adherence to rules when in command.

In theory, state colleges were required by the terms of their charter to sponsor a training battalion among the student body. In practice, most of them, including the University of Nebraska, did not. Student cadets seldom drilled or studied military subjects; they had no interest in them and, due to custom and habit, expected not to be bothered by such distractions. Their marching skills were poor, their uniforms wrinkled, their shoes unpolished. No one thought the U.S. Army would be fighting another war anytime soon, so there seemed little point in going to all the trouble to prepare. Officers assigned to these training programs tended to agree with this assessment and considered the idea of transforming students into soldiers a lost cause. Commanders went through the motions of recruiting and training without any delusion that they could actually produce a functioning military unit.

Into this sleepy, sloppy state of affairs marched Second Lieutenant John J. Pershing. He was somewhat familiar with the school because two of his sisters had attended there. He believed he could make real soldiers out of the lackadaisical boys on the company roster. Even the chancellor, James H. Canfield, had wondered if the military potential in his students could be tapped. Pershing knew he could do it.

Students shuffling in for drill on Pershing's first day must have been awestruck by the change. Previous cadet commanders had expected little of them. This fellow expected everything. He looked and acted every inch the leader, standing straight and tall, shoulders square, uniform perfectly tailored and immaculately clean. He had a clear, strong, slightly raspy voice that seemed to carry a country mile. After calling roll once, he evidently remembered the name of everybody in the ranks. He missed no detail, accepted no excuses.

Far from being affronted, the cadets loved him for it. Unit pride swelled to levels previously unimaginable. Student-soldiers eagerly took on the challenge of pleasing this difficult but inspiring taskmaster. If they met the standards of "the lieut [*loot*]," as they called him, they knew they'd done their best and more. The corps of cadets mushroomed from 90 members to 350. Some of them spent so much time polishing their gear and practicing drill that other professors complained they were neglecting their studies. Chancellor Canfield replied that the professors ought to join the corps themselves. One of the university regents agreed, saying, "I told the faculty that there was not a study in the curriculum that in my opinion meant half so much to these young fellows [after graduation] as their military training under Pershing."[6]

The chancellor and his preteen daughter, Dorothy (who became Dorothy Canfield Fisher, an acclaimed children's author and educator), admired Pershing's abilities and enjoyed his company. Pershing biographer Gene Smith wrote that they "found the lieut off-duty to be a charming man with a light touch and an irresistible, friendly smile."[7] Pershing made many friends, including

Charles G. Dawes, a young lawyer from Ohio who would become one of his closest confidants. The two of them often met for inexpensive meals at a neighborhood lunch counter and shared many adventures, including jumping out a window to escape police who had raided an illegal boxing match. In November 1892, Pershing celebrated his promotion to first lieutenant with a night of heavy drinking among friends. The six of them resolved to form a Nebraska battalion of their own, but their plan evidently didn't last past the hangovers.

With the cadet corps running successfully, Lieutenant Pershing told Chancellor Canfield he needed more to do. Canfield assigned him to teach mathematics and fencing at the university's prep school, further restoring him to the teaching role he left ten years earlier to get an education of his own. This led to a story young Dorothy enjoyed telling over and over again as an adult. Pershing did his classroom teaching dressed in civilian clothes. One day after the cadet corps had assembled for inspection, commandant Pershing marched out with his uniform in perfect order as always—and a derby hat on his head. Returning the adjutant's salute, he realized his mistake as he put his hand where his cap bill should have been. Without a word he marched off the field, changed hats, marched back on, and continued the drill.

Pershing wanted a select group of volunteers to compete in a national drill team competition in Omaha. The winner received a gold cup and fifteen hundred dollars. Forty-five students signed up to practice before and after class every day. They called themselves the Pershing Rifles. At their final practice they performed beautifully, drawing applause and cheers from the competition audience that was watching. The students' reaction was too self-congratulatory and smug for Pershing, who cancelled their night on the town, drilled them some more, and sent them to bed at nine o'clock as punishment for showing off.

The next morning, as the Pershing Rifles made their final preparations, the lieutenant told them he thought they were going to win. His prediction came true. When the winner was announced, the Lincoln crowd that had come to cheer them on rushed the eight-foot fence between the stands and the parade ground, Chancellor Canfield climbing over with everybody else. Of Pershing, the chancellor later declared, "I say without the slightest reserve that he is the most energetic, active, industrious, competent, and successful officer I have ever known . . . thorough in everything he undertakes, a gentleman by instinct and breeding, clean, straightforward, with an unusually bright mind; and peculiarly just and true in all his dealings."[8]

Along with his duties as commandant and math teacher, Pershing realized a lifelong dream at Nebraska by earning a degree from the university law school. Impressed, the inspector general of the army sent Major E. G. Fechet to learn more about this high-achieving lieutenant and his methods. Fechet's glowing report said in part,

> Too much credit cannot be given to [the] commandant. The high degree of efficiency is due entirely to the energy, ability, and tact to organize and command of Lieutenant Pershing . . . I doubt if there can be found a better drilled battalion outside of West Point. I know these are high words of praise, but I feel

confident that any officer of experience, after seeing the battalion, would confirm my opinion.[9]

Lieutenant Pershing's tour of duty in Nebraska ended at the end of the school year in 1895. He wondered whether this was a good time to leave the army and pursue his law career. He was thirty-five and still a first lieutenant. The army remained almost an afterthought in national affairs. They hadn't fought a major war in thirty years and might never fight another one. His friend Charles Dawes was a lawyer but far from successful. Seeing Dawes struggling despite his obvious ability and hard work, the lieutenant decided this was not the time to forgo a steady paycheck and a measure of security for the financial uncertainty of a civilian law career. If he stayed in the army, the question remained how to advance through the ranks. Pershing thought he might be promoted faster if he had a staff position rather than a line command and applied for transfer to the quartermaster corps. The request was denied. Even so, he decided to stay in the army.

His cadets were sorry at the thought of losing him. When classes ended in the spring, they asked their commandant for a pair of his uniform pants, which they cut into souvenir ribbons for each member of the corps. Pershing said his farewells in Lincoln and in October reported to Fort Assiniboine, Montana, where a new chapter in his military career was about to begin.

THREE

Cuban Campaign

" BLACK BOYS IN blue." That was what the black soldiers in the Tenth Cavalry Regiment were called by other troops, though they were more widely known as "Buffalo Soldiers." Cheyenne warriors said they fought like buffalo; survived wounds the way buffalo did; and had long, curly hair like buffalo. Pershing's new duty station with the Tenth at Fort Assiniboine, in the High Plains of Montana not far from the Canadian border, was a world away from the cadet parade grounds of Lincoln. Here he further refined his leadership skills and gained experience in military command.

All of the officers in the Tenth were white. Army regulations specified that they discipline colored soldiers with a firm hand, since they were assumed to be less self-controlled and capable than their white counterparts. Pershing treated black troops fairly, though with his customary insistence on obeying regulations to the letter. He once knocked an enlisted black man into the river for disobeying an order, not because he was black but because he disobeyed.

There was very little for the men to do, and the assignment was for the most part uneventful and boring. One of the few sorties Pershing had out of Fort Assiniboine was to intercept a tribe of Cree Indians heading south and return them to Saskatchewan, in accordance with a treaty agreement between the United States and Britain. In spite of the inaction, Pershing learned to recognize and appreciate the commitment and resourcefulness of his black soldiers.

Army commander General Nelson A. Miles, who had been so troubled by the massacre at Wounded Knee, came for an inspection visit and brought two prize hunting dogs with him. Lieutenant Pershing organized a hunt to Fort Beauford and the Yellowstone River, where the party slept in tents banked with snow and had a wonderful time shooting deer and prairie chickens. Impressed by Pershing's obvious energy and ability, Miles had the lieutenant transferred to six months of temporary duty in Washington DC as his *aide-de-camp*. Though there were military matters to attend to, Pershing spent much of his time in Washington escorting the general's wife and daughter on social calls, including a visit to Mrs. Grover Cleveland at the White House.

In 1897 when his tour in Washington was finished, Pershing became an assistant instructor in tactics, equitation, and cavalry training at West Point. Here the lieutenant was in his element, poised for even greater success than before. He had done wonders molding the cadet corps in Nebraska. Now with such well-trained and dedicated students to start with, it should be possible to set new standards of excellence and be revered by his command in the same way the Pershing Rifles had idolized him.

Instead, the cadets at West Point despised him. To them he seemed impossibly rigid, merciless, and always ready to lash out at the slightest infraction. He missed nothing and criticized every fault no matter how small. It may have been that as a West Point alumnus himself, he held these men to a higher standard than he had others. It was also true that, unlike at Nebraska, he seldom mixed with his command except when he was commanding them. They never saw the fun-loving, hard-drinking officer who had once jumped out of a window to dodge the police. They saw only the flinty taskmaster, never satisfied, quick to mark a demerit. He came across as, in biographer Gene Smith's words, a "heartless martinet."[1]

Sworn to a strict military code of honor, cadets had little recourse for expressing themselves. One of the most extreme forms of condemnation, rarely used because of its severity, was "silencing." The cadets invoked it against Pershing. When he entered the mess hall every cadet stopped talking and stopped moving, leaving him to navigate his way in absolute silence through a frozen sea of staring faces. The mark of silencing followed an officer from the first instance onward; it could even derail his military career by branding him, fairly or not, as one who could not earn genuine respect from his men. Lieutenant Pershing paid absolutely no attention to the slight, continuing his inspections and criticisms exactly as before.

A traditional way for cadets to pass judgment on tactical officers was to give them nicknames. Sometimes these were marks of respect or endearment—but not in Pershing's case. In light of his command of black cavalrymen in Montana, they scornfully christened him "Nigger Jack."

Pershing didn't care about the nickname. What he did care passionately about was the fact that America was going to war with Spain. In 1895 the U.S. government supported a native uprising in Cuba against the Spanish colonials who had ruled them for centuries. The revolt had come when it did in part due to a financial crisis after America put a tariff on sugar, the lifeblood of the Cuban economy, the year before. Spain sent General Valeriano Weyler y Nicolau to restore order on the island. He dealt harshly with the Cuban people, sending thousands of them to concentration camps.

President William McKinley believed the United States had no business engaging in a standoff with Spain over Cuba, regardless of how badly General Weyler treated the natives. He did send the battleship *Maine* to Havana in January 1898, however, as a precaution to safeguard Americans there and to stand by in case evacuation became necessary. On the night of February 15, 1898, the *Maine* exploded in Havana Harbor with the loss of 274 officers and men, most of them asleep in their quarters. Opinion leaders in the States demanded the United States retaliate for the sinking. Senator Redfield Proctor of Vermont declared on the Senate floor that America should declare war on Spain. Pressure to strike back mounted even as doubt surfaced whether the *Maine* hit a mine or blew up on its own. The question was never settled: investigations in 1974 and 1999 failed to solve the mystery.

Regardless of the facts, news barons Joseph Pulitzer and William Randolph Hearst used their New York papers, the *World* and the *Journal*, respectively, as megaphones for shouting a call to arms. War was good business for them because it made news, and news sold papers. The American heartland came much to the same conclusion about war on its own, though not for the sake of selling newspapers. Strengthened by decades of peace and relative prosperity, the United States felt insulted by Spain. Flexing its colonial muscle and stirring up such unrest had cost American sailors their lives. The United States had to retaliate; these American deaths could not go unanswered. On April 20, 1898, McKinley signed a joint congressional resolution demanding that Spain pull out of Cuba, which the United States declared independent of Spanish rule. On April 23, Spain declared war on the United States. Two days later the United States reciprocated, retroactive to April 22.

The Spanish-American War quickly expanded into America's first worldwide military exercise. Not only were Americans determined to fight Spain for Cuba, they also attacked the Spanish colonial outpost of Puerto Rico, southeast of Cuba past the island of Hispañola. U.S. forces concurrently challenged the Spanish in Guam and the Philippine Islands on the other side of the world. While the army prepared for war in the Caribbean, Admiral George Dewey led an attack force of six American ships from China to fight the Spanish fleet at the Philippine capital of Manila. Beginning his assault at dawn on May 1, Dewey destroyed the entire Spanish fleet in a single morning. The Spanish surrendered shortly after noon at the cost of one American life, a sailor who died of heatstroke.

As America's first appearance on the international military stage unfolded, Pershing and every other officer were determined to join the fight. They were soldiers and this was war—the first war to come along in a generation. None of them wanted to sit on the sidelines, no matter how valuable their teaching skills were to the army. They were disappointed, then, to learn that no one assigned to West Point could request reassignment to the battlefield. The Academy needed its experienced instructors in the classroom and on the parade ground now more than ever.

Naturally, officers immediately began angling to get around this directive. Pershing contacted everybody he could think of asking for any duty in the field, even leading National Guard volunteers. His superior in the equitation department was the brother of a New Jersey congressman, but that avenue proved a dead end. Chancellor Canfield from Nebraska, now president of Ohio State, wrote President McKinley on Pershing's behalf. Pershing even considered resigning his commission to join the volunteer cavalry unit being raised by the assistant secretary of the navy, Theodore Roosevelt. Pershing had met Roosevelt when he was police commissioner of New York and had found they had much in common, including a love of the American West. Now here was this wealthy businessman and politician preparing to lead his men in battle while Pershing, a career officer, fidgeted impatiently on the banks of the Hudson far from the action.

The lieutenant's way out was through George D. Meiklejohn, assistant secretary of war. Meiklejohn had been a congressional representative from Nebraska, where he and Pershing became friends. Pershing had encouraged Meiklejohn to apply for the assistant secretary post, and recommended him to Pershing's old commander General Miles, who had the ear of the president.

Now Pershing wrote Meiklejohn in desperation: "May I be relieved from here? George, I could no more keep out of the field than I could fly."[2] While the secretary of war, Russell A. Alger, was out of town, Assistant Secretary Meiklejohn reassigned Pershing. The lieutenant returned to his previous command of the "black boys in blue," serving as quartermaster for Buffalo Soldiers of the Tenth Cavalry bound for Cuba.

It was an open question whether or not America was justified in fighting the Spanish. There was no question, however, that the American army was woefully unprepared. There were still fewer than thirty thousand officers and men in uniform. None of them under fifty had any battlefield experience. Many were scattered across the continent in isolated outposts when war was declared, so that getting them to Eastern seaports was a major operation. There were no plans, facilities, or equipment in place to support large troop movements; no way to buy, transport, and warehouse the food, medicine, ammunition, horses and mules, and countless other items necessary for waging war. Whatever small, antiquated, hopelessly overworked systems there were became overwhelmed by politicians trying to do favors for their constituents demanding a certain assignment, or no assignment, or the chance to sell their wares to the War Department.

Lieutenant Pershing met the Tenth Cavalry camped at Chickamauga National Park in Georgia, where the ever-observant young officer got a taste of what was in store in Cuba: unreliable supplies of bad food, tainted water, and miserable living conditions. Local shopkeepers would not serve the black soldiers, adding to the inconvenience and irritation. When a barber refused a black soldier a shave, the soldier left the shop and shot the barber dead through the window. Enlisted men were confined to camp for the rest of their stay. The Tenth moved on to their embarkation port of Tampa, where vast strings of railroad cars filled with Cuba-bound supplies sat idle on the sidings. The cars had no bills of lading, so someone had to go through every crate in every car to inventory its contents. Stymied by poor planning and bureaucracy, Pershing and other officers broke into railcars and warehouses and took what their men needed.

In May, Pershing was promoted to captain. As part of the First Cavalry Division, he and the Tenth sailed for Cuba on June 7. Days later they landed without resistance from the Spanish, though inept planning again caused serious problems. There weren't enough small boats to ferry all the men to shore. Trying to swim to the beach, a number of soldiers drowned under the weight of their equipment. Horses and mules were shoved overboard loaded with supplies. Some made it to dry land; others swam the wrong way and disappeared, a loss of both the animal and its cargo.

Anxious as he was to join the assault, Pershing was assigned to stay on board as his ship went to pick up three thousand Cuban freedom fighters eager to help the Americans. Only about a thousand were actually on hand, and their appearance astonished Pershing, who described them as "a rag-tag, bob-tailed, poorly armed, and hungry lot in appearance anything but an effective fighting force. We had to give them food and all we could get out of the hold at the time was hard bread and sugar, which they ate ravenously . . . We got little or no help during the campaign from this or any band of Cuban *insurrectos*."[3]

Pershing landed on the beachhead at last. He had not missed any significant action because the commanding general, William Shafter, delayed his attack until more supplies were brought ashore and his men were better organized. President McKinley had chosen Shafter for the Cuban campaign over Pershing's friend General Miles because the president knew Miles had political aspirations and the president didn't want to risk a victorious general running against him for reelection in 1900.

Scrambling to field an army on short notice, the United States assembled an assault force reflecting its emerging position as a melting pot of races and cultures. The three infantry brigades and two cavalry brigades included everything from teenage farm boys to Civil War veterans old enough to be their grandfathers. The Tenth Cavalry Regiment—black "Buffalo Soldiers" with Captain Pershing as their quartermaster—were there along with the Twenty-fourth Colored Infantry.

Serving in the First Brigade was former assistant navy secretary Theodore Roosevelt, who had resigned his office to be second in command of the First U.S. Volunteer Cavalry, the Rough Riders. He was average height, about five feet eight inches, and still reasonably trim for a man nearing forty. Roosevelt was powerfully built, in excellent condition, and sat his horse with comfortable ease. His pince nez, fair complexion, and refined speech gave him a somewhat bookish appearance, but his grit, energy, and natural ability made him an admired and respected leader. His life experience, ranging from cowboy to New York City police commissioner, made him comfortable around men of any rank or social status. Early in his deployment his regimental commander, Colonel Leonard Wood, was promoted to brigadier to replace the sick brigade commander. Roosevelt then assumed command of the Rough Riders.

The immediate American objective in Cuba was a rise held by well-protected Spanish defenders. San Juan Hill and nearby Kettle Hill formed the two high points of San Juan Heights, a low ridge on the outskirts of Santiago, Cuba's second-largest city. The plan was to take the Heights and then move quickly into Santiago, where a fleet of Spanish warships lay offshore. Americans would attack the city, forcing the navy to send its ships to sea, where the waiting U.S. Navy would capture or destroy them. Though the Spanish were vastly outnumbered, they had a secure position, heavily fortified from long years of skirmishing with the Cubans, and they had much better weapons.

Technology was becoming increasingly important in warfare, and in this the defenders had the upper hand. Their German Mauser rifles fired bullets at supersonic speeds, making a cracking sound as they flew and giving them deadly accuracy. Gravity causes bullets to drop at the same rate regardless of their velocity; the faster the bullet, the less it drops before reaching its target. In addition, the Spaniards' rapid-fire breech-loading cannon were far superior to the slower-firing American artillery and used smokeless powder where the Americans' did not.

The American attack began with an artillery bombardment early on the morning of July 1. The Tenth marched forward at 8:30 a.m. into some of the most inhospitable terrain imaginable for cavalry operations. Cavalry troops in Cuba often traveled dismounted because of the impenetrable jungle and because there was a chronic shortage of horses. The path through the tangle of tropical growth was narrow, rough, twisting, and flanked by thick vegetation.

As soldiers approached the Aguadores River near the Spanish lines, an American observation balloon floated overhead. Balloons had been used since the Civil War for map making and to locate enemy troop and artillery positions. The American spotters in Cuba were thus carrying on a long military tradition in pinpointing the Spanish defensive deployment. This intelligence would have been particularly helpful where tropical growth blocked the view from the ground. The problem was that as the balloon hovered over American lines, it showed the Spanish defenders exactly where the Americans were. Americans screamed curses skyward as Spanish soldiers opened fire, cutting down American troops in what Pershing called "a veritable hail of shot and shell."[4] Someone in the balloon yelled down, "They're firing on you!" Another stream of curses filled the air from furious troops below as the balloon was finally hauled down. There had been no time for the balloonists to gather any useful information, only time to give the Spaniards an easy target.

Against the Spanish army's modern Mauser rifles, most Americans carried relatively ineffective bolt-action Krag Springfields or old-fashioned single-shot Model 1873 Springfields that used black powder cartridges. Once the Americans started shooting, smoke from their rifles further defined their positions. Another hazard to the U.S. forces, as the day dragged on, were their regulation wool uniforms, torturously hot as the tropical sun rose higher. Men started dropping from heat exhaustion.

Only the volunteer Rough Riders under Roosevelt had proper outfits: khaki uniforms, canvas leggings, and wide-brimmed hats against the merciless sun. Drawing on influential friends in Washington, Roosevelt had done what he could to see that the Rough Riders' equipment was as good as possible. He secured modern Winchester rifles for his officers, and a private donor gave the volunteers two gas-powered Colt-Browning machine guns that could fire 450 rounds a minute.

Both Pershing's and Roosevelt's regiments fought under General Wood in the Second Cavalry Brigade. Early in the day, progress was stalled by heavy enemy fire. As the battle intensified, some of the Seventy-first New York Volunteers threw down their arms and turned tail, abandoning their posts. There was no room for them on the road, which was choked with oncoming traffic, and the jungle was impenetrable. So they lay down in the middle of the trail. Pershing's men, Roosevelt's Rough Riders, and other advancing units stepped over and on top of the deserters as the advance continued.

A squadron from the Tenth had gotten separated from the rest and Pershing went back to find them. As he searched he came upon his division commander, General Joseph Wheeler, sitting on his horse in the river while bullets drilled into the water around him. A West Point graduate and former Confederate general, "Fighting Joe" was the rare rebel who had been invited back into the U.S. Army. President McKinley offered him a new commission after Wheeler had served more than fourteen years in the House of Representatives.

General Wheeler was a short, wiry man, now past sixty,

bald and with a long white beard. He was dangerously sick with malaria but insisted on being with his men during their advance. As he saluted, Pershing recoiled from the shock of a shell landing between the two of them, sending up a plume of water. The captain was surprised to see the old leader in the thick of the fighting. It was lesson he never forgot: a fighting general stays with his men.

Pershing found the lost squadron and led them back to the front. Spanish soldiers laid down such thick fire that the Americans were stalled in the high grass in front of a heavily fortified blockhouse on San Juan Hill. An attack seemed suicidal, but there was no way they could retreat back along the narrow trail or through the jungle.

As the halted Americans endured relentless shelling and small arms fire, Colonel Roosevelt, among others, thought they would be slaughtered where they stood unless they took action. He believed they had to make an all-out charge; even a gradual advance would be too deadly. A captain told him there were no orders to move out. Finally, seeing that he was the highest-ranking officer in sight, Roosevelt gave the order to advance and then led his men up San Juan Hill, dismounting along the way. Roosevelt would be recommended for the Medal of Honor for his heroic actions that day. Denied at first, probably because of a letter he wrote criticizing the military for needlessly exposing troops to malaria, the medal was awarded posthumously by President Bill Clinton in 2001.

Orders for the Tenth Cavalry to advance came after a lieutenant, Jules Ord, asked General Hamilton Hawkins for permission to call the charge. Hawkins answered, "I will not give permission and I will not refuse it. God bless you and good luck." The lieutenant's immediate superior, Captain John Bigelow Jr., gave Ord the honor of sounding the call. When the order came, Pershing led his men forward, the black soldiers fighting bravely and suffering high casualties. "We officers of the Tenth Cavalry could have taken our black heroes in our arms," he said later. "The men took cover only when ordered to do so and exposed themselves fearlessly."[5] Whatever he felt inside, to his men Pershing exuded the confidence of a fearless leader absolutely sure of himself. As he positioned his men while under heavy fire, one West Pointer thought he was "as cool as a bowl of cracked ice."[6]

In the end, American Gatling guns were the critical advantage to taking San Juan Heights, raining thousands of rounds a minute down on the Spaniards as the assembled American troops mounted a massive charge. The defenders dropped their rifles and ran. Recalling the moment years later in his memoirs, Pershing wrote, "In the elation that followed this achievement men cheered, shook hands with each other and threw their arms about each other, and generally behaved wildly regardless of rank." He also noted the compassion his men had for their defeated opponents: "A colored trooper gently raised the head of a wounded Spanish lieutenant and gave him the last drop of water from his canteen."[7]

Captain Pershing impressed the officers who saw him in action that day. One of them, Colonel Theodore Baldwin, sent him a note that said, "I have been in many fights in the Civil War, but on my word you are the coolest and bravest man I ever saw under fire in my life."[8]

Spain quickly gave up the fight for Cuba. Far greater menace to the Americans than Spanish bullets were disease and depriva-tion. As the torrid summer season advanced, thousands of men came down with malaria, yellow fever, and dysentery. Pershing became critically ill with malaria, alternating severe chills with a raging fever. Supply problems continued: spoiled meat, unsafe drinking water, and severe shortages of tents and medical supplies. Despite his own miserable sickness, Pershing foraged and appro-priated what he could for his men, collecting clothing, blankets, food, and other necessities without requisitions or official sanc-tion. His experience as a quartermaster of the Tenth repeatedly reinforced to him the crucial importance of organization, pre-paredness, supplies, and equipment to an army's success.

On July 17 the Spanish surrendered and on August 14 the Tenth Cavalry sailed for New York and a well-deserved rest. "Our regiment has done valiant service," Pershing wrote his friend, Assistant Secretary of War Meiklejohn. "No one can say that colored troops will not fight."[9] Stateside, Pershing faced another manner of conflict when the army charged him as unit quarter-master with a million dollars' worth of equipment and supplies that were unaccounted for. A friendly lieutenant insisted that the returning soldiers held about that same amount of surplus gear they had not been issued. An inventory proved him right, and Pershing was cleared.

Captain Pershing went to visit his parents in Chicago. While there, he saw his family doctor who said his case of malaria was "alarming." Next, the army sent him on an inspection tour of Western forts that had been drained of troop strength to fight in Cuba and simultaneously against Spanish forces in the

Philippines, Guam, and Puerto Rico. America controlled all these far-flung places now, raising a host of questions about local civil and military laws, taxes, administration, municipal services, banking regulations, and much more. Meiklejohn summoned Pershing to Washington to discuss these matters. The captain had a law degree and had proven himself industrious and capable. Furthermore, while native Cubans had welcomed the American forces that pushed out the Spanish, Filipinos scorned them. The Moro people in the southern part of the Philippines especially despised the new foreigners.

There was only so much Pershing could do from Washington to suggest policies for the Philippine Islands. Meiklejohn wanted him to go there to develop ways to govern this new American territory. Pershing's old friend Charles Dawes, once a struggling lawyer and now a wealthy businessman and highly placed friend of President McKinley, encouraged him to stay in Washington. If he wanted steady promotion, he needed to get involved in army politics. Possibly remembering how his friend General Miles was snubbed for his political aspirations, Pershing decided he would much rather be in the field than behind a desk.

En route to his new posting, Captain Pershing visited London, Paris, Rome, Cairo, and Ceylon. He landed at Manila. and then sailed six hundred miles south to Zamboanga, a city of twenty thousand on the Philippine island of Mindanao. It was New Year's Day 1900 when the lieutenant stepped ashore into a world of colonial Spanish architecture, ancient native customs and prejudices, new American ambition, and unprecedented personal challenge.

FOUR

Mastering the Moros

FILIPINOS RESENTED AND resisted their new American overseers at first, even though the United States assured them that America only wanted to improve their lives, not to treat them as inferiors. Their experience as a colony of Spain conditioned them to expect exploitation for their labor and resources rather than the schools, roads, hospitals, and waterworks the United States promised. As the American military and civil authorities settled in, the majority of Filipinos began to feel a measure of acceptance and trust toward them. The exception was the population of Mindanao in the southern part of the country. All Filipinos shared the same Malaysian ethnic background and language. The difference was that while the rest of the Philippine population was overwhelmingly Catholic, most inhabitants of Mindanao were what were known as "Moro," from the Spanish word for Moor, indicating their Islmaic faith. Moros were Spanish-speaking Muslims who scorned their Christian countrymen in the north and despised Americans even more.

Pershing described them:

> The Moro is of a peculiar make-up as to character, though the reason is plain when considered, first, that he is a savage; second that he is a Malay; and third, that he is a Mohammedan. The almost infinite combination of superstitions, prejudices and suspicions blended into his character make him a difficult person to handle until finally understood . . . He is jealous of his religion, but he knows very little of its teachings.[1]

Moros recognized no government, local or foreign, and were organized into tribes of a few hundred each headed by a chief called a *datto*. They practiced polygamy and slavery. Some warriors filed their teeth to points. Their prize possessions were razor-sharp weapons handed down from one generation to the next: the kris, a long double-edged dagger, sometimes with wavy edges, designed for lethal stabbing; the campilan, a two-edged sword wide at the tip and narrow at the hilt; and the barong, a keen-edged cleaver for chopping off limbs, with which a skilled warrior could cut a man in two at the waist with a single swing.

The Moros fought other Moro tribes and even attacked each other, but their most virulent aggression was against Christians. Young men became *juramentados*, oath-takers, who swore an oath to kill as many non-Moslems as possible and earn a guaranteed place in paradise when they died. The more they killed, the richer their reward in the afterlife would be and the greater the number of pure and voluptuous women waiting to greet them there. This enticement led to tragic results. *Juramentados*, high on pain-numbing drugs, their bodies shaved and wrapped tightly in white strips of cloth, strapped a kris to each arm and went on rampages, butchering as many people on a roadside as possible before being killed themselves. Captain Pershing wrote of an officer who emptied his revolver into a Moro attacker and was still hacked to death. The U.S. Army adapted the Colt .45 revolver specifically to stop these Moro fanatics.

As he had done with Native Americans in the West, Pershing—alone out of all the American officers in the Philippines—set out to learn about the Moros. He would rather negotiate with them than kill them, and to do that he had to gain their trust. He studied their language, traditions, and hierarchies as no other white man had. Though the animosity gradually died down between American troops and other Filipinos, the rage and violence of the Moro went on as before. There was no central authority to deal with, no avenue to negotiation, and no effective appeal to a people who took human life so lightly.

Pershing spent his first few months in the Philippines on administrative duties. The military governor of the islands, General George Whitefield Davis, learned to depend on him for advice in dealing with the Moros. As time passed, General Davis saw no improvement in relations with the Moros even as the rest of the islands grew more peaceful. He decided his only chance at pacifying the Moros without destroying them was to turn the matter over to Captain Pershing. The heaviest concentration of Moro tribes was east of Zamboanga near the town of Iligan and Lake Lanao, where the Moros had built fortified strongholds around the lake and prepared to fight to the death.

Davis sent Pershing to Iligan with two companies of his cavalry regiment and three companies of infantry. His orders were to contact the Moros and make friends with them. It would be his first field command in the islands, and as he started out the captain must have recalled what his regimental commander said about soldiers newly arrived from the United States: "I have a hundred horses that have never seen a soldier, a hundred soldiers who have never seen a horse, and a bunch of officers who have never seen either."[2]

Captain Pershing took charge of the post at Iligan on October 11, 1901. His first order of business was an inspection, which turned up a disastrous state of disorder and uncleanliness. The parade ground was overgrown with weeds; soldiers loitered aimlessly outside their dirty, tumbledown quarters. As the captain entered the mess hall ramrod straight, walking with precise, ordered steps, his uniform immaculate as always, the cook snapped to attention. Pershing took a frying pan from its hook and ran a white-gloved finger over the bottom. The fingertip turned black with grease. Without a word the captain slid the pan across the floor at the cook, who remained at attention except for jumping up to avoid getting hit. Pershing tested every other pan and utensil the same way, sliding the dirty ones toward the increasingly nervous mess sergeant. When the captain picked up the meat cleaver and shot the cook a glance, the enlisted man bolted for the door. Pershing stopped him with a word and then told him there would be another inspection in a week.

During that week the post at Iligan was transformed. Pots and pans in the kitchen shone like silver. Uniforms were trim, boots polished, faces shaven, and living quarters neat and clean. As soon as his command was up to standards, Captain Pershing turned all his energy to understanding and befriending the Moros. He sent messengers and letters to the tribal *dattos* introducing himself and explaining how he wanted to work with them, not against them, to make better lives for their people. When Moro families came to Iligan on market day, Pershing milled around in the crowd, greeting men and women, asking about their crops and their children. "They liked to talk and wanted to speak with someone in authority," Pershing observed. "In this they were given every encouragement."[3] The captain ordered his men to go out of their way to be polite to the natives. He bought firewood and other supplies from them, and he encouraged soldiers to buy their market goods. He hired Moro laborers at a fair wage.

The Moros were suspicious. Why would the Americans offer to build roads and bridges and buy from them without demanding something in return? Pershing patiently and consistently carried out his plan, reaching out to the natives, earning their trust. Finally one of the most important *dattos*, Manibilang, sent his son to meet with Captain Pershing. The captain sent the young man back with a personal invitation to his father. Later they exchanged letters.

Pershing must have considered it a great victory when Manibilang himself arrived for a visit. He came on horseback with a slave walking on each side, one carrying a gold-handled kris and the other a box of betel nuts, buya leaves, and lime—the *datto*'s version of chewing tobacco. Ahead and behind him were guards with rifles, which they bought from Chinese traders, though the Moros were notoriously bad shots. The entourage also included family members, advisers, and other slaves, all dressed in brightly colored clothes—tight jackets and divided skirts for the women, flowing blouses and pantaloons for the men.

The *datto* stayed three days, each filled with long meetings where the chieftain asked questions about America and the army's intentions. Would he make the Moros wear hats like the soldiers'? Manibilang asked, touching his own regal turban. Would the women have to wear skirts? Would he force them to eat pork? Pershing did his best to answer as fully as possible.

Pershing patiently explained that he wasn't there to impose American customs on them, though he tactfully avoided discussion of slavery and polygamy. His aim, he insisted, was to help the Moro people by improving education, communication, and trade. The visit was a turning point in relations with many of the Moro tribes. Manibilang spread the word to other *dattos* that Pershing was a man of his word and his intentions were worthy. Other leaders came to meet him, and the captain redoubled his letter-writing campaign to keep them abreast of his plans and operations.

Manibilang then did what no *datto* had ever done: he invited an American to visit him. He asked Pershing to pay a return call on him at his camp. Townspeople and his own men told Pershing it was a trap. The Moros would lure him into the jungle and then slice him to ribbons. The captain thought otherwise, unwilling to let the historic opportunity pass by. He went unarmed, accompanied only by an interpreter and native scouts. Arriving at camp, it seemed as if the whole tribe had come to welcome him to the *datto*'s home, a large timber building with plank floors and a palm thatch roof. He was guest of honor at a feast. He reported that

> I have never tasted more delicious chicken, seasoned as it was with native herbs, and the rice, steaming hot, was cooked to perfection . . . None of the women of the house sat with us but the senior wife directed the serving in a quiet, dignified voice . . . I do not recall ever having seen a Moro wife or child abused in any way. No child, even by concubine or slave, was regarded as illegitimate.[4]

The next day Captain Pershing took a tour of the countryside by *vinta*, a dugout canoe with bamboo outriggers, then returned to Iligan with a forty-man honor guard. He had shown the Moro leader that American interests and objectives in the Philippines were far different from what the Spanish interests had been. "From that time," Pershing later wrote,

> Manibilang was not only a warm personal friend of mine but an earnest advocate of friendly relations between Americans and Moros. In the months to come he rendered much valuable assistance in dissuading other dattos from opposition. With the exception of a few groups, the Lanao Moros in general [all the tribes living around Lake Lanao], largely through his influence, became friendly. The word spread of the good business

that could be done at Iligan and the security afforded all Moros there and the number of people who came to market steadily increased.[5]

The invitation from Manibilang inspired other *dattos* to host visits from Pershing, and he accepted every offer. Wherever he went, he stood by his resolve always to travel unarmed. On one trip he noticed his orderly had tucked a pistol under his shirt. "Lanckton," the captain said, "a soldier's word is more important than his gun."[6] He ordered the gun left behind. In his forays to various native camps, Pershing adapted to local custom when he could, politely deferred when he could not, and continued answering an endless string of questions about Americans and their objectives.

Preparing for bed at a *datto*'s home one night, Pershing was visited by his host and "a most attractive member of his harem who, he advised me in the most matter-of-course manner imaginable, would accompany me. The announcement rather took me aback for a moment and my embarrassment was undoubtedly apparent, but I managed to express my thanks and declination without giving offense, the datto sending the woman away as nonchalantly as he had brought her in."[7]

On another trip, he answered questions about Americans' religious beliefs. Personally, Pershing showed no strong inclinations toward or away from religion, though as a soldier and officer he surely knew the power of faith in inspiring and encouraging men on the battlefield. Moro leaders queried him about whether every American believed in the same God. If there was one God, how could there be so many different religions? Were Americans circumcised? If they were, how could Moros live with them since Moros were not? No question was too strange or too complex for the captain to try and answer.

Even as Captain Pershing built his reputation for trust and fairness, some Moros stole guns and other items from the army and cut their telegraph lines. When *dattos* or their retainers insisted they couldn't control wayward tribesmen, Pershing replied that as leaders it was their responsibility to discipline subordinates. They should command their followers as Pershing commanded his. Leaders could delegate authority but not responsibility. The same captain who showed endless patience during a native conference was ruthless in dealing with his own soldiers when they disobeyed. Told that two enlisted men developed cholera after drinking at a spring he had ordered off limits, he barked, "Let them die! They disobeyed my orders."[8] Both soldiers did die.

Captain Pershing knew some of his fellow officers disapproved of the way he accommodated the natives. Though he had made remarkable headway in befriending and pacifying the Moros, there were still tribes south of Lake Lanao who resisted any move toward reconciliation and peace. While the majority of natives now trusted and accepted Pershing, these *dattos* and their followers were more violent than ever. Colonel Theodore Baldwin, commander of a camp near the trouble zone, preferred a show of force to continued negotiating. Determined to crush the opposition once and for all, he attacked a *cotta*, or fortified camp, at the settlement of Pandapatan. *Cottas*, some of which had held off the Spanish for three hundred years, had massive walls up to twenty feet high and nearly as thick, surrounded by moats lined with sharpened bamboo spikes.

Baldwin ordered a direct assault, which failed and cost him fifty men. He planned a second attack for the next day, but the Moros melted into the jungle during the night. The day after that the departmental commander, General Adna Chaffee, reassigned Pershing to Baldwin's camp, newly christened Camp Vickers in honor of the first soldier to fall at Pandapatan. Chaffee put the captain in charge of all Moro-related operations, which included most of what went on.

Baldwin and Pershing were already friends and had a cordial working relationship. Baldwin continued to argue his position that confronting Moros with force was the right approach, however, while Pershing held out for patient progress through negotiation. When it became clear that Baldwin was going to pull rank and insist on fighting, General Chaffee convinced the War Department to promote the colonel and transfer him stateside. Captain Pershing assumed command at Camp Vickers.

Several more months of meetings and messages convinced Pershing that three *cottas*—Maciu, Bayan, and Bacoclod—would never listen to reason, never trust the Americans, and never be subdued except by force. Furthermore, some of the Moros he had previously won over began asking themselves why, if this American was so strong and powerful, he then sat in his camp while native bandits harassed travelers and sent snipers to take potshots at his men.

Captain Pershing decided he had to act before his new native friends lost confidence in him. His first target was Maciu, where two *dattos* and their followers were barricaded in. When the natives refused his last offer to talk, he marched on them with seven hundred men. Surprised by a counteroffensive outside of Maciu, Pershing organized his troops and called up artillery. The Moros ran, but in trying to follow them Pershing realized his fieldpieces and supply wagons could never negotiate the jungle terrain ahead. Unwilling to send his men forward without proper support, he retreated.

A week later he was back, this time with a detachment of engineers to build a road through the dense vegetation. By nightfall the Americans had the *cotta* surrounded on three sides. Pershing intentionally left the fourth side open so any natives who wanted to could leave safely. The captain wasn't interested in killing this enemy, only in showing other resistant *dattos* his power. In the middle of the night, a band of Moros attacked and Americans answered with deadly fire; meanwhile the other natives escaped, leaving their fortress empty. Pershing burned the previously unassailable *cotta* to the ground. The results were a wave of new Moros eager for peace and a big drop in the number of attacks against Americans.

Bayan was the next objective. The local Muslim holy man, Sajiduciman, insisted to other Moros that since Americans were Christians and ate pork, anyone who welcomed them would go to hell. Pershing's letters to Sajiduciman went unanswered. When Pershing explained that war was the only choice remaining, the imam invited him for a visit. On February 10, 1903, Pershing set out for the *cotta* with a combined force including artillery, but feared as he approached Bayan that he might be dangerously outnumbered. He saw what looked like hundreds of Moros gathering there, dressed in their finest, most colorful clothes, which were saved for special occasions, including the wearer's death.

Sajiduciman took the captain on a tour of his fortifications. Pershing answered with a drill showing off his men's firepower. Then the host led his visitor to a circle of elders squatting around a copy of the Koran. There he told the captain that the assembled leaders had voted to make him a *datto*. It was a historic moment never to be repeated: an American military officer acclaimed as a Moro chief. Pershing managed a short speech on peace and friendship. From then on he was honored as a leader by Moros across the island. Men asked him to settle disputes, women came to have their marriages blessed, and children were named after him and wrote him letters addressed to "My Father."

American newspapers hailed the "ideal administrator of consummate skill" bringing the "privileges and beneficences of Anglo-Saxon civilization" to the island people. The *New York Sun* reported, "No other officer has been more frequently or more favorably mentioned. Every few days we hear of his preaching the gospel of peace to some new *datto* out in the wilds of Mindanao. Interspersed with these accounts, others come to tell of his subjugation of some rebellious *datto* whose greatest need is just such a parental spanking as Pershing bestows upon him."[9]

But "a parental spanking" had no effect on the *datto* of Bacoclod. In answer to one of Pershing's letters he sent back a charred reply:

This letter goes to you burned in six places to indicate that it means war. You should not be here, for you are not like us. You eat pork. If you do not wish to leave this region, come and live in Bacoclod under the sultan [another translation for *datto*], who will practice circumcision on you.[10]

Pershing tried once more, writing to Bacoclod and sending copies of the message to surrounding native landholders:

We have not interfered with the customs, habits, government or religion of any Moro. We have demonstrated to the whole world that we are not here to make war nor dispossess the inhabitants of Lanao of anything that is theirs. Two or three dattos refuse our friendship simply because, as they say, they do not like Americans. To those dattos I say that if they continue their opposition they must some day suffer the consequences of their stubborn ignorance.[11]

Pershing left Camp Vickers on April 5 at the head of a large force of infantry, cavalry, and artillery, including mortars and heavy but effective water-cooled Vickers machine guns, along with hundreds of pack animals carrying supplies. Troops marched ten miles in a day through intermittent tropical downpours, halting to eat their customary field rations of canned salmon—which the troops called "goldfish"—and hardtack. As they camped that night beside Lake Lanao, Moros infiltrated their bivouac and shot two soldiers. The second day the Americans came to the *cotta* and formed their battle line about half a mile from the massive outer walls and surrounding moat.

Pershing planned the same assault as before, a fierce artillery bombardment followed by small-arms fire on three sides, leaving one side open for escape. It took time to position the men and caissons in the rain and mud. Pershing set the big guns to their work, firing until dark. Under cover of night, some defenders took advantage of the escape route and left, along with their women and children. The next morning under a flag of truce, the *datto* offered to surrender if his men could keep their weapons. Pershing refused and the battle resumed. By nightfall the *cotta* had been pounded to rubble and the infantry had crept close enough for a final assault. Pershing decided to wait through one more night in case more Moros wanted to run for their lives. When the sun came up, the war flag flew from the ruins.

Pershing's men rushed the fortress, crossing the moat on a bridge of bamboo. When the bridge collapsed, the invaders used it as a ladder to climb out of the moat and up to the gates. Americans fired their weapons continuously and threw burning grass and wood into the compound. The Moros' gunpowder stores exploded, leveling what remained of the building and marking the beginning of the end of the fight. Natives who held their ground died to the last man, about sixty killed where they stood and the same number fatally wounded. Pershing had no deaths among his command and only a handful of wounded.

The army surgeon in the field that day wrote with admiration:

Had Pershing assaulted on the first or second day, the casualties would have been terrible on our side. By pounding the cotta with artillery and giving its people a chance to escape, he so intimidated the Moros, that when he finally assaulted there only remained in the fort the really desperate characters who were determined to die fighting . . . How much different would have been the result had he listened to the impetuous advice of his officers.[12]

When the victorious Americans returned to Camp Vickers, the garrison commander requested the entire expedition be quarantined in tents outside the fort in case some of the soldiers had been exposed to cholera. Pershing agreed that the rest of the men shouldn't risk cholera, but his troops were tired and deserved their comfortable quarters after such hard fighting. His solution was to move the soldiers who had stayed behind out into the quarantine tents so his men could sleep in their own beds.

The Moro resistance was broken. As a symbol of victory and a show of force, the new department commander, General Samuel S. Sumner, assigned Pershing to lead a force completely around Lake Lanao, the geographic center of the longest and fiercest opposition to the American presence and to the Spanish before that. No Westerner had ever completed the circle. Until Pershing negotiated his settlements with the majority of *dattos* and defeated the rest, it would have been far too dangerous to attempt. Any non-Muslim would have faced Moro warriors sworn to keep them, as infidels, out of their territory.

The captain took five hundred soldiers and a handful of Moro guides, departing camp on May 2, slogging through dense undergrowth and fetid swamps. Though there were a few small pockets of resistance, most of the natives they met cheered, waved, and flew white flags. In some communities, Pershing's march around Lake Lanao became the event that anchored their calendar—a certain event was said to have been so many years before or after Pershing's march.

The Lake Lanao expedition arrived back at Camp Vickers on May 10, exhausted but elated. In three hundred years no Spanish army had done what they had. All of the tribes had to allow Pershing and his men safe passage in order for them to go fully around the lake. By completing the circle, Pershing proved he had subdued every major Moro settlement and that the scattered network of Moro leaders and their people acknowledged him as their friend. The march marked the end of Pershing's tour of duty. The Philippine climate aggravated the malaria he had caught in Cuba, and the army decided it was time to send him home. American newspapers speculated he would soon be promoted.

Pershing sailed for America, arriving in San Francisco on July 30, 1903. On December 7, his old friend Theodore Roosevelt, elevated to the presidency by the assassination of President McKinley two years earlier, weighed in on the matter of his promotion. In his annual message to Congress the president said, "When a man renders such service as Captain Pershing rendered last spring in the Moro campaign, it ought to be possible to reward him without jumping him to the grade of a brigadier general."

In certain cases, a captain could be promoted directly to brigadier, jumping over all the majors, lieutenant colonels, and full colonels waiting ahead of him. Nearly forty-three, Pershing was one of the oldest captains in the army, though not nearly the most senior according to time in grade. The president could promote soldiers out of order, but only to the rank of general officer. Roosevelt was recommending the captain for a higher rank, at the same time admitting the president's hands were tied unless he bestowed a general's star.

General George Davis, supreme commander in the Philippines, seemed ready to welcome Pershing to the highest echelon:

> When the time comes for the Department to make the selection of general officers for promotion from the rank of captain, I hope that Captain Pershing may be selected for brigadier general. I have frequently brought his merits to the attention of the Department, in routine and in special communications, for gallantry, good judgment, and thorough efficiency in every branch of the soldier's profession. He is the equal of any and the superior of most.[13]

The Pershing family residence at Zamboagna, with its wide verandahs, lush tropical views, and a dining room that seated sixty.

On the night of August 26, 1915, an ember from the fireplace ignited fresh varnish on the floor of the Pershing home at the Presidio, near San Francisco. Pershing was in Texas. His wife and three daughters died; his son Warren was rescued through an upstairs window (arrow).

The Library of Congress

After fire claimed his mother and sisters, Warren Pershing spent as much time as possible with his father. When they were apart, Warren's letters were always put on top of the general's stack of mail.

FIVE

"Banzai, Jack!"

CAPTAIN PERSHING WAS assigned to the army staff in Washington, where he enjoyed celebrity status for his march around Lake Lanao and the fact that the president had praised him before Congress. His fame brought more social invitations around the capital than he could accept. Pershing had been known as a ladies' man and an excellent dancer at West Point. Despite his reputation in the field as a harsh and impersonal commander, he was a gracious guest who enjoyed the company of women. And they enjoyed his.

As he grew older his round, boyish face had taken on a chiseled silhouette and his sandy hair became lightly flecked with gray. His sharp chin, firm jaw, and piercing eyes, along with a thick, full mustache, contributed to his image as a handsome and imposing man whether in uniform or civilian clothes. One of the social outings he generally attended was the weekly dance at Fort Meyer, just across the Potomac from Washington near Arlington Cemetery.

At the Fort Meyer dance on December 9, 1903, Captain Pershing met Helen Frances Warren, "Frankie" to her friends, the daughter of Wyoming Senator Francis Emroy Warren. Warren was chairman of the Senate Military Affairs Committee and, except for a two-year break, had been in the Senate since 1890. Before that he was mayor of Cheyenne, governor of Wyoming Territory, and the first governor of the state after Wyoming joined the Union. He had come west from Massachusetts after the Civil War, during which he served as an infantry volunteer and received the Medal of Honor. The senator was a cattle-man, owner of hundreds of thousands of acres of ranchland, an investor in Cheyenne's first municipal electric lighting system, a mercantile businessman, and the richest man in Wyoming. He looked every inch the successful businessman and politician: solidly built, with short gray hair parted in the middle, pince nez on a black silk cord, and a large handlebar mustache.

Frankie Warren had graduated from Wellesley only a few months earlier, but was already making a name for herself as a Washington hostess. Her mother died when Frankie was in high school, and young Miss Warren took charge of many of the society duties expected of her family. She made social calls on her father's behalf and received visitors to their suite in the Willard Hotel, then and now one of the finest hotels in town, only a short walk from the White House. Her official duties did not keep her from the full social life of a very wealthy and well-connected young lady. She was not beautiful in the conventional sense. Her features were strong, not delicate, her fair skin framed by curly, dark hair. She was a woman of the West—independent, athletic, and confident. She was also a woman of Washington refinement and social graces.

Frankie was a vivacious and popular young woman in the capital. Her diary for 1903 describes a steady diet of dances, dinners, shopping, dress fittings, evenings at cards or the theater, late nights, and leisurely mornings. Despite her wealth and position, she was fun-loving, warm, and full of imagination and vitality. She had been engaged, but broke her engagement on November 30 during her fiancé's visit to Cheyenne. On December 7 she was at the Capitol for President Roosevelt's address to Congress and his glowing praise for one particular captain's service in the Philippines.

Two nights later she met that captain. Afterward she wrote in her diary: "Went to a hop at Ft. Meyer with Papa . . . *Perfectly lovely time*. Met Mr. Pershing, of Moro and Presidential message fame." That same evening, Pershing woke up his friend Charles Magoon, later governor of Cuba and then of the Canal Zone, exclaiming, "I've met the girl God made for me!"[1]

On December 11 Frankie wrote that she "had dinner with the Millards to see Capt. Pershing. It was *just great*. Have lost my heart."[2] A week later: "Went to dance at the Navy Yard. All the Navy and military [were] there and all the swells of the city. Danced every dance but one and have lost my heart to Capt. Pershing irretrievably. Perfectly elegant dancer."

Two days before Christmas he sent her flowers. In her thank-you note she invited him to the theater with her and her father. The night before the play, December 29, the two were at the same dance when it started to snow. Pershing handed Miss Warren into her carriage then started to walk home on the snow-covered sidewalk. When Frankie offered him a ride, he replied that it wasn't proper for anyone at the party to see them leaving together unchaperoned. "All right," she said. "Walk ahead down to the corner. I'll pick you up there."

This whirlwind romance continued by letter in the new year, as Pershing was posted to Oklahoma and Frankie went home to Cheyenne. Though his closest friends knew Captain Pershing was capable of genuine affection, many more would have been astonished at the thought that this stern taskmaster who had wooed more than his share of ladies over the years, a bachelor at forty-three who had never shown any interest in marriage, was head over heels in love with a rich college graduate twenty years his junior. But he was smitten and so was Frankie.

As their courtship continued by mail, she was the one insisting they should get married while he held back. For one, he was worried about the differences in their financial status. Her father was a millionaire many times over and she had an income of $10,000 a year—nearly a quarter million dollars today. Published pay scales put Pershing at $2,600 annually, about $65,000 today, as a captain with between fifteen and twenty years of service.

The difference in their incomes didn't bother Frankie. On the contrary, she considered it an advantage since with all her money, it didn't matter how much the captain had because she would always have enough for them both. "Let me tell you right here, you dear old Jack Pershing," she wrote, gushing with love and youthful exuberance, "that you might just as well stand in the middle of a field and wave a red flag at a bull as to flaunt the word 'obstacle' at me. Here I am just urging and urging you to marry me. It seems that I have done nothing else since last February, and I am getting discouraged with you. I am going to bend all my efforts to fall in love with every attractive man I meet. Please may I kiss your nose?" She teased him about buying her an engagement ring. "If worst comes to worst, one can be procured along with a stick of candy for one cent—and I'll lend you that much."[3]

In August 1904, he visited her and her family at their ranch. He wrote later about kissing her there for the first time: "I never kissed your lips until we both said we loved each other. I should not have done so under any other circumstances. That kiss, as all others have been, was attended with feelings that to me are divinely sacred."[4] On Christmas Day in Washington, Captain Pershing asked Senator Warren for his daughter's hand. The senator already had seen it was love at first sight and happily gave his consent.

The couple's plan for a June wedding was complicated when, two days after they became engaged, Secretary of War William Howard Taft summoned Pershing to say he was recommending him as military attaché to the American embassy in Japan. Pershing and Taft knew and respected each other from the captain's service in the Philippines when Taft was the civil governor there. The ambassador in Tokyo had requested a bachelor who played bridge for the post. Pershing said he didn't play bridge well and that furthermore he'd just gotten engaged.

"You're not married now, are you?" Taft asked.

No, Pershing said, he wasn't married yet.

"You have the appointment," Taft declared. "What you do afterward is your business."

Japan was at war with Russia, and the War Department wanted Pershing at his new duty station right away. His wedding to Frances Warren was rescheduled for January 26, 1905. In spite of the mere month between engagement and ceremony, the event was the highlight of the social season. Senator Warren sent out forty-five hundred invitations and the church was packed to overflowing even as a blizzard swept through Washington. The Senate delayed its session that day so that members could attend. *Washington Mirror* magazine printed Frankie's photo on its cover and the captain's inside. The bride wore a gown of white satin with sleeves of lace and chiffon, her tulle veil crowned with a coronet of orange blossoms. The captain wore his dress uniform, as did his fellow officers serving as ushers. Pershing could scarcely believe what was happening. To his wife he wrote soon after, "I am the happiest man in the world and have the dearest, loveliest wife . . . Wife and sweetheart in one, and all mine."[5]

Typical for a man who kept his emotions to himself, Pershing said little publicly about the service at Epiphany Episcopal Church or about his religious beliefs in general. He clearly felt with all his heart, as he had told his friend Magoon, that God had made his new wife just for him. Yet while religion was interwoven into the social fabric of the military and of the Washington political set, it was not a matter the captain spoke much about.

It took two banquet halls at the Willard to hold all the guests for the wedding breakfast. The newlyweds headed west, stopping to see the Pershing family in Chicago and the Warrens in Cheyenne. An incident while he was there tellingly revealed the captain's approach to leadership. One day the captain rescued an eight-year-old girl being dragged by a horse. When she balked at getting back on, Pershing picked her up, sat her in the saddle, and followed her home. He told her if she hadn't remounted she might be afraid of horses afterward. "If you have a fall—mental, moral, or physical—pick yourself up and start over again immediately. If you do, in the long run life won't beat you."[6] Though far from the battlefield, it was a textbook example of Pershing's leadership philosophy: People who overcome small setbacks with resolve and personal bravery will handle big challenges equally well. Success in great affairs results from the habit of driving oneself to success in the smallest details.

Captain and Mrs. Pershing sailed on February 14, arriving in Yokohama March 5. Though Frankie had spent the trip miserably seasick, the couple went on to Tokyo that night, where they attended a dinner hosted by the Japanese war minister for Lieutenant General Arthur MacArthur. The general had sailed over with the Pershings, sent by the U.S. government as a military observer. MacArthur, one of the highest-ranking officers in the army, had been military governor-general of the Philippines when Taft was civil governor but had been reassigned stateside after repeated clashes between the two.

The Japanese were winning the war, though there was fighting left to do. Pershing heard people on the street shouting, "Banzai!" an expression of enthusiasm—"yay" or "hooray"—derived from the phrase "ten thousand years" and implying a wish for "long life to the emperor." Four days after they arrived in Tokyo, Captain and Mrs. Pershing embraced on a platform where a private railroad car waited to take Pershing and General MacArthur to the front lines in Manchuria. It was "the saddest of goodbyes" for the captain. Frankie, ever the enthusiastic optimist, waved as the train pulled out and yelled, "Banzai, Jack!"

Except for one short furlough back to Tokyo, Pershing spent six months in the field shadowing Japanese troops, looking at the primitive conditions of the country and marveling that his hosts had defeated the Russians. Until the mid-nineteenth century, Japan had been locked in feudal isolation. There had been no trade or communication with the West, no development of transportation, agriculture, or manufacturing for centuries. At the turn of the twentieth century the country remained undeveloped; rural roads were still mostly muddy ruts carrying carts pulled by oxen or human "coolies," as they were called.

Yet Japan developed an army that had unexpectedly defeated the powerful Russian Empire. The Russians wanted an all-weather seaport on the Pacific Ocean. Conflict simmered for years before Russia tried to force Japan into accepting its control of Manchuria. Czar Nicholas II never expected the Japanese to stand up to his renowned army. Yet, not only did they resist, the Imperial Japanese forces took the offensive, successfully besieged the contested city of Port Arthur, and all but destroyed the Russian navy.

This was the first "modern" war in that it used the machine guns and entrenched defenses that would play such an important role in the European war a decade later. These innovations attracted military observers from around the world, including Pershing and MacArthur. Americans had been badly outgunned in Cuba during the Spanish-American War, and American Gatling guns had been crucial in turning the tide in the battle for San Juan Heights and Santiago. Now the United States military wanted to see the effects of contemporary weapons, including heavy battleships, and of modern tactics, especially the use of entrenched infantry protected with machine-gun batteries and long-range artillery.

The main fighting was over by the time the two Americans landed at Tokyo, leaving only mopping-up action before the Treaty of Portsmouth ended the conflict. The treaty was signed September 5 at the Portsmouth Naval Shipyard in Maine, another symbol of America's growing world influence and military might. Pershing's friend President Theodore Roosevelt invited representatives from both sides to his home at Oyster Bay, New York, and conferred with them separately and together as they hammered out an agreement. Roosevelt received the Nobel Peace Prize the following year for his work, though he declined the large cash award that came with it, saying it would be like taking money for rescuing a drowning man.

Pershing was frustrated that his Japanese hosts kept him from what little action there was, and thus distracting him from gathering useful military information. He participated in a Buddhist ceremony honoring the war dead, visited a veterinary hospital, and saw abandoned battlefields strewn with unburied bodies and shattered equipment. The government supplied him with a horse, groom, rickshaw, and servants. The Japanese field marshal invited him to a banquet of *foie gras* and chicken. Pershing wrote to Washington, knowing the letter would be intercepted, and said that the Japanese were keeping him away from anything important and that he might as well be elsewhere. His complaint stung his secretive hosts and brought a change in policy. The next day he accompanied a reconnaissance detail that skirmished with Russian cavalry.

Pershing made a number of friends on the trip. American correspondent Frederick Palmer thought the captain was the "most pleasingly human and companionable" person he met in Manchuria. Whoever he met and whatever he was doing, Pershing thought constantly about his devoted wife. Being apart so soon after their wedding was hard on them both. He poured his heart out to her in letters, the taciturn soldier clearly captivated by a kind of love he had never known before: "Frankie the fact is we should never be separated, it is too hard. Let's go back to Wyoming and go on a ranch and ride the range together, let's settle down in some place where our lives can be spent for each other."

Yet he knew that he could never give up a soldier's life no matter how he longed to be with her. "I have been reading today of those brave old soldiers of our own Civil War, and I really couldn't be anything but a soldier. Well: I must go to bed. Come to bed darling. Ah, and take me in your arms and hold me tight to you, press my cheek on your breast and kiss my hair. Sweetheart darling, dearest wife—I love you, love you, good-night."[7]

Captain Pershing scrutinized every detail of the Japanese

military with tireless energy. He sent reports back to Washington on everything from observation balloons to the pension system; military police, the medical corps, and postal service; the rate of wear on gun barrels and the dimensions of pontoon boats. Considering the aftermath of the Russo-Japanese War, Pershing concluded that winning a modern war depended upon seeing and understanding the situation at hand on a far larger scale than a single battle, or even a single campaign as in the past. Long-range weapons, telephone and telegraph communications, and other innovations had made war a long-distance operation, scattered over an immense area and involving massive numbers of troops. Maneuvers were too huge and the effective range of weapons too long for a single commander to mastermind and execute a plan of attack.

These observations reinforced lessons from his battlefield experience. In the Philippines he had seen firsthand the power of firm yet patient negotiation with the Moros; the more he could engage the enemy in talk, the less shooting he had to do. In Cuba the military objectives were far easier to achieve than mastering the endless minutiae of supply, organization, transportation, and coordination. These had been more destructive foes than the enemy soldiers. Certainly personal bravery, endurance, patriotism, and sacrifice were still essential to military success. For those attributes to be fully and effectively applied, however, they had to stand on a foundation of solid, comprehensive planning: administration, preparation, and attention to detail.

With the end of hostilities, Pershing returned to his posting in Tokyo where he and Frankie settled into their house in the

American colony near the embassy. The Pershings attended a reception hosted by the emperor and had the special honor of hunting with his majesty, chasing after tame ducks with large hand nets. A group of American dignitaries came to visit, including Secretary Taft, Senator Warren, and President Roosevelt's daughter Alice. Frankie traveled with them to the Philippines, where she toured Camp Vickers. She was shocked to meet Moro children who called Captain Pershing their father, until she realized it was an honorary title.

The Pershings rented a second home on the beach at Hayama, where the translucent paper doors slid open to reveal breathtaking views of Mount Fuji. As the captain described it, "When the moon shone and light breezes rustled through the pines and caused the temple bells to tinkle, my wife and I felt that peace was as near about us as we should ever find it on this earth."[8] Their happiness was multiplied by the birth of their first child, Helen, on September 8, 1906.

Less than two weeks later, what should have been another joyous change in their lives got off to an unsteady start. On September 15, President Roosevelt promoted John J. Pershing from captain to brigadier general. Frustrated that Pershing had not been promoted by the army and unable as president to name any but general officers, Roosevelt took the only step he saw possible to bestow the rank he believed Pershing deserved. At a single stroke Pershing went from one of the oldest captains in the army—it was two days after his forty-sixth birthday—to one of the youngest generals.

Pershing received his general's star by jumping ahead of

862 officers with more time in rank, and every one of them was unhappy. The press had a field day with the news, accusing Pershing of trading on his position as son-in-law of a rich and powerful senator who was also chairman of the military affairs committee. Editors dredged up his old nickname as a West Point instructor, writing that Nigger Jack Pershing led his black Tenth Cavalry troops under Roosevelt in Cuba—may in fact have saved the colonel and his Rough Riders from defeat—and now as president, Roosevelt was returning the favor. The truth was that other generals had recommended Pershing's promotion, and there had been precedent set by several similar cases of a captain being elevated directly to general.

Senator Warren and the president exchanged letters about the matter. Roosevelt published his, which declared, "The promotion was made solely on the merits, and unless I am mistaken you never spoke to me on the subject until I announced that he had been promoted. To promote a man because he marries a senator's daughter would be an infamy; and to refuse him promotion for the same reason would be an equal infamy."[9]

Potentially far more damaging was the rumor that surfaced claiming Pershing had kept a concubine in the Philippines, which was a common practice in Mindanao at the time, and had had two children by her. Newspapers reported that Frances was considering divorce. Pershing categorically denied the charges. Of the three "witnesses" supposedly confirming the charge, one was dead and the other two publicly denied the story. Captain Thomas Swobe, who lived in the same building with Pershing in the Philippines, affirmed, "We walked together, rode together—drank from the same bottle, and I know Pershing as any man living knows him. And no more honorable, upright, manly and soldierly man than Pershing ever wore soldier straps. And I am ready to defend him against any charge his enemies may bring . . ."[10]

Pershing was out of town when the news broke. Frankie wrote to him immediately: "You know that my love is the same whether it is true or not. If they are able to substantiate the charges, I would love you more than ever because your need of me would be greater." She also fired off a note to her father: "You stand by Jack, no matter what infamy may be said of him."[11] With a little time and perspective the controversy died down, though rumors of a Filipino mistress followed Pershing for years afterward.

SIX

Pacific Odyssey

FOUR MONTHS AFTER his promotion, General Pershing was back in the Philippines as commander of Fort William McKinley near Manila, the largest American command outside the United States. He relieved Colonel Henry Kingsbury who, like many other officers at the fort, outranked Pershing until recently. Kingsbury had graduated West Point fifteen years ahead of Pershing. Surely it was awkward at first because so many of the general's subordinates were older and more experienced, and because his father-in-law was who he was. If it made Pershing uncomfortable, it made no difference whatsoever to Frankie. She embraced her social duties as wife of the commanding officer with her trademark friendliness and energy, quickly making friends with the other wives.

General Pershing soon realized that his brigade was unprepared for war. Few of the officers had any idea how to plan and execute large-scale maneuvers. He instituted training programs to condition his units to working effectively together. Pershing suggested to his superior, General Leonard Wood, that all brigades serving the Philippines rotate through Fort McKinley for training. Wood turned him down, citing operational inconvenience. Pershing's program would have been priceless to the officers and men who in a very few years would fight "the war to end all war" in France. As biographer Jim Lacey observed, "Tens of thousands of American doughboys paid the ultimate sacrifice for the neglect of training in favor of expediency."[1] Wood, trained as a doctor, had served as personal physician to presidents Cleveland and McKinley. His lack of insight and concern on this point is all the more puzzling in light of the compassion and understanding he demonstrated in the practice of medicine.

While Pershing embraced the big picture in commanding large forces, he never ignored an opportunity to reprise his role as a teacher. The best lessons were often taught by example. The general once assigned a young engineer to build a bridge across a river. The lieutenant said the assignment was impossible because the water was too high to get the first rope across. When the lieutenant got an order, Pershing explained, it was his responsibility to find a way to execute it. Pershing insisted he never gave an order he couldn't carry out himself. To illustrate the point, the general tied the rope to his own saddle and swam his horse across. Those who witnessed it never forgot Pershing's lesson.

The general and Mrs. Pershing welcomed their second

daughter, Anne, in March 1908. As his assignment came to an end, Pershing again considered leaving the service to spend time with his growing family. Occasional separations from Frankie during her pregnancy were almost more than he could bear. "Frank," he wrote, "I am not going to stay in the service away from you. D--- the service. D--- everything and everybody that takes from me or ever has taken from me one minute of your time or one thought of your mind. Oh, Frances, I need you every moment. I cannot live without you. And I shall not try. It is only half a life. It's so incomplete, so aimless."[2]

The army called Pershing back to Washington. Four hundred well-wishers attended their going away party at Fort McKinley. The general, worn down physically by the strain of the tropics, turned the trip home into a vacation. The family of four sailed west to Hong Kong and Japan on August 1. Accompanied by a Japanese maid, they landed at Vladivostok to catch a train bound across Siberia for Europe.

The general had an American bank draft for travel expenses. Once he paid for the tickets, baggage porters, and everything else, he had three rubles left—equal to $1.50. That was all the money he could get until the train reached Moscow in ten days. With his hungry girls crying and the maid scowling at him, Pershing took a box of fine cigars down the coach to a Danish naval officer he had met on the ship from Japan, hoping to barter them for cash. The fellow traveler heard the general's story with a chuckle and then extended him a loan until they arrived in the Russian capital.

Along the way the family marveled at the desolate steppes, dense forests, veiled Muslim women, colorfully dressed gypsies, dashing horsemen, and other exotic sights. They spent a week and a half sightseeing in Moscow. Little Helen celebrated her second birthday with a cake, toys, and new clothes; five days later, on September 13, the general turned forty-eight. The family continued to St. Petersburg, Warsaw, and Berlin, where the Pershings called on the brother of a German officer he'd met in Manchuria and visited his artillery regiment. Two weeks in Berlin convinced the general that Germans were the most regimented people he had ever seen and that their army was trained and drilled to a level of "perfect preparation" unmatched anywhere in the world. Their discipline would make the Germans a formidable foe in battle, Pershing believed, and their organization and training would produce an awesome fighting machine.

Back in America at last, the Pershings moved into the Willard Hotel in Washington where Senator Warren lived when he was in town. The general felt rested from his tropical assignment and, in fact, hoped to go back to the Philippines as civil governor of the Moro province he had done so much to tame years before. His health remained unsteady, however, and he had had a German specialist examine him for a heart irregularity. Rumors circulated that he would have to take medical retirement.

After President Taft's inaugural ball, Pershing went to a health sanitarium in Watkins Glen, New York, for three months, followed by a month at a military hospital in Hot Springs, Arkansas. His doctor there, West Point classmate Major George Deshon, ran him through a battery of tests and reported, "In my opinion and in that of my associates there isn't a . . . thing the matter with you."[3] He took Pershing horseback riding at seven o'clock the next morning. The general maintained a daily regimen of plenty of sleep, healthy diet, two hours on horseback, and forty minutes of calisthenics followed by a massage and an hour nap.

Meanwhile, Frankie had gone to Cheyenne to prepare for the arrival of their third child. Pershing rejoined his family in June 1909 when his wife gave birth to their first son, named Francis Warren Pershing after his grandfather. By the fall of that year, all five Pershings were back in the Philippines where the general now wore two hats: one as civil governor of Moro Province, and the other as its military commander. He held both the civil office he had wanted and the military position his previous experience and success so well prepared him for.

He relished the dual assignments because of his interest in the Philippine people and took the matter of wearing two hats literally. He had separate offices for each job, most days spending time in both. At his military office he wore his uniform; in his civilian office he wore civilian clothes. The family had a magnificent official residence on the beach near Zamboanga, surrounded by palm trees and orchids, with wide verandas and a dining room that seated sixty. They were attended by a small army of drivers, grooms, watchmen, maids, cooks, housekeepers, and aides to keep them comfortable and help with entertaining.

Pershing took advantage of every opportunity to include his family in his official duties. One highlight of their time there was attending the funeral of the Japanese emperor. President Taft especially encouraged Frankie and the children to go. Taft's official representative, Secretary of State Philander C. Knox, picked the Pershings up en route to Tokyo. The children created a sensation on the streets of the Japanese capital, three tow-headed, round-eyed little figures riding in a rickshaw.

When he and his family were apart, Pershing missed them more now than ever. His love for Frankie knew no bounds, and now with three children—Helen, Anne, and Warren—his sense of loss was multiplied during their absences. Mrs. Pershing and her brood made return visits to Japan to escape the tropical climate, and even made the long voyage home for a visit to Wyoming. The general always wrote his wife faithfully, pouring his heart out and plumbing the depth of his emotions in a way he never did publicly. "To the sweetest, dearest woman in all the world," he wrote to her in Cheyenne. "I am mighty lonesome for you. Last night, I simply gave way and couldn't keep back the tears. My Heavens, I simply worship you."

His wife returned the sentiment, struggling to capture the intensity of her feeling on the page: "My own darling, darling Heart—my great lover—oh, Jack, I just go mad for love of you—I adore you. I love you from the top of your dear curly head to the very end of your toes!"

At home the general was as happy and comfortable as a man could be. In the field, it was a different story. Pershing was disappointed to see that so much of the progress he had made in earning the Moros' trust and building the community had started to unravel. The top commander in the Philippines, General Leonard Wood, did not share Pershing's preference for patience and negotiation but dealt with natives using an iron hand. Wood, who was about Pershing's height of six feet, with a triangular face and trim mustache, had a taciturn streak evidently untempered by the sort of patience and selflessness that characterized Pershing. As military governor of Cuba, he had ordered the head of a local newspaper and the paper's cartoonist jailed for publishing an unflattering cartoon of Wood. There was also friction remaining between the two generals from Pershing's criticism of Wood during the charge on San Juan Hill, when Wood had proposed retreat. Strong resolve was necessary in dealing with the Moros, Pershing thought, but it had to go hand in hand with sound judgment and respect for the other man's viewpoint.

Pershing believed the core of the problem between Americans and the Moros was that the natives were split into so many tribes and factions that they couldn't live peacefully among themselves. Rather than try to sort out all the connections and identify specific opportunities for collaboration, the Americans stayed in their bases, isolated from the locals. "Bringing them thoroughly under control, to terminate warfare among them and lead them to a better way of life was an undertaking never seriously attempted," the general observed. "The work required careful judgment and continual patience as well as force and the willingness to use it."

General Pershing continued with the methods he had used successfully before—talking with the people, listening to their concerns, looking for a negotiated solution, leaving bloodshed as a last resort. American soldiers had treated the Moros harshly in recent years. "Though force has to be used to a certain extent," he admitted, "and to the utmost limits when dealing with criminal elements, it was clear that there had been too much haste in using arms to enforce laws and regulations that ran counter to age-old customs."[4]

Pershing saw there was much work ahead. He started small. When a tribe refused to accept Pershing's recommendation for settling a boundary dispute, he challenged them to a baseball game. If they won, they could handle the dispute in their own way; if the Americans won, they had to take Pershing's recommendation. Pershing played third base and the Americans prevailed. The Moros accepted the settlement. Not only did the natives avoid a fight, but Pershing's stock rose in the community as well. Many remembered him from his posting at Camp Vickers that ended with the legendary march around Lake Lanao. They remembered he was a trustworthy soldier who cared about them and treated them fairly. Pershing set out to fan these still-burning embers of respect and confidence.

The general went on a tour across his Kentucky-sized province to visit with the *dattos*, some of whom welcomed him as a returning hero. When he arrived, one of his first orders was to move soldiers out of the forts, where they were separated from the natives, and into small units scattered across the region. This encouraged interaction between Americans and the locals, diffusing the mutual mistrust that had cropped up over the years. At every stop on his journey, Pershing repeated his promise that the Americans were not there to push the Moros off their land but to help them.

The general moved from troop redeployment to an ambitious program of building roads, warehouses, electric plants, clinics, and schools. He hired Moro laborers whenever possible; some natives even volunteered their services in order to take part. In February 1911 Pershing organized the biggest trade fair in the history of the Philippines, staged in a block of temporary bamboo buildings hung with electric lights. Electricity was one of the sensations of the fair for the Moros, along with an automobile, a battleship in the harbor they could tour, and a merry-go-round.

Some of the tribes wore elaborate, brilliant clothes, while others were naked except for feathers and jewelry. The scene was a kaleidoscope of coats decorated with seashells, ruffled trousers, tight-fitting body suits, giant headdresses, and tinkling silver ankle bells. There were dances, foot races, horse races, diving exhibitions, tugs-of-war, parades, cattle shows, and more. Groups that started the day wary or suspicious of each other were soon fast friends. Not only did the forty tribes have an opportunity to barter with each other and with the Americans, the often-isolated groups had a chance to get to know each other. They discovered they were actually far more alike than they were different. And as Pershing well knew, the more they understood about each other, the less likely they were to fight. It was one of the most richly rewarding teaching moments of the general's life.

Pershing rode through the grounds in his car, acknowledging the unbridled cheers of twenty thousand spectators. As he passed the reviewing stand, *dattos* he had fought years before at Lake Lanao threw their turbans in the air and applauded wildly. He waved back at them, the tears welling up in his eyes.

For all his success, there were two nagging problems in Moro Province. One was the northern Filipinos' encroachment on the Moro culture. Moros despised the Catholic Filipinos on the larger northern island of Luzon. Catholics were the majority in the country overall, but only about 10 percent of the population in Moro Province. Northern Filipinos saw the defeat of their

Spanish overseers as an opportunity to extend their influence to the Muslim Moros in the south. One old and respected tribal leader encouraged Pershing not to abandon his people to the Filipinos. He wanted American rule and peace among tribes. But if Filipinos tried to take over, he vowed to fight. Pershing promised not to abandon the Moros to northern domination.

The second and far more serious problem was the attacks of Pershing's old foes, the *juramentado* zealots, Islamic oath-takers whose goal was to kill as many non-Muslims as possible. Mixed in with them were common bandits that used some of the same tactics, though without the religious fervor. The *juramentado* were especially dangerous not only because of their fanaticism, but also because they would attack crowds, cutting or killing several victims at once. As in the past, studying his enemy led to a solution. Knowing the killers' hope of more rewards in heaven and also the Islamic revulsion to pigs, Pershing endorsed one form of dealing with oath-takers that proved extremely effective. It was a clear example of using the power of religion as a military tool, underscoring Pershing's understanding of the influence of faith and of knowing as much as possible about the enemy. As he described it:

> These *jurmentado* attacks were materially reduced in number by a practice the army had already adopted, one that the Mohammedans held in abhorrence. The bodies were publicly buried in the same grave with a dead pig. It was not pleasant to have to take such measures but the prospect of going to hell instead of heaven sometimes deterred the would-be assassins.[5]

The general decided that the b
tion was to take away their weapons.
would be an impossible policy to impleme.
Pershing from his plan. These weapons—the
the rest—were prized possessions of the Moros,
handed down through the generations. Even so, on .
8, 1911, General Pershing issued a proclamation that the
would have until December 1 to turn in their weapons for cu
pensation. After that, the Americans would disarm them by force.
When resistant Moros killed a soldier and wounded three, the
general realized the time for talking had run out.

Pershing led the counterstrike against the Moros himself. His
wife and children were at a camp in the highlands, away from the
tropical heat and humidity. "I would give anything to end this
business without much fighting," he wrote Frankie. "But the
Taglibi seem vicious. They have shown their teeth and snapped
at us. You can't talk a fellow around to much of anything if he is
shooting at you all the time."

Pershing wrote to the resistant *dattos*. As he had years earlier
during his Lake Lanao offensive, he gave them one last warning, a
final chance to avoid bloodshed.

All Moros are the same to me as my children and no father
wants to kill his own children. Now, I am writing you that you
may know that I want my children to come in and stop fighting. We do not want any more killing. Too many Moros and
their women may be killed. Your people are better off not to
have guns as we can then have peace. The government will

,y for all guns. If you [are] leading men to not stop fighting, ,ou will be responsible for the lives of your women and children ... Give up the guns and save your own lives and the lives of your people.[6]

Instead of surrendering their blades and guns, the Moros retreated with their families to a fortified *cotta* on a mountain called Bud Dajo. When they had done the same thing four years earlier, General Wood immediately called in artillery and pounded the blockhouse to rubble, leaving no escape route for the natives and no time to use it if there had been. The Americans lost eighteen soldiers killed that day, while more than six hundred Moro men, women, and children died. Pershing chose differently. He surrounded the compound and waited. Eventually the Moros started surrendering in small groups. Soldiers captured the *cotta* in one final firefight with a loss of about a dozen natives killed, no women or children among them; three Americans were wounded.

That left one massive concentration of holdouts. An estimated ten thousand Moros assembled in a huge *cotta* atop an extinct volcano called Bud Bagsak. From there they staged attacks on other Moros, who had turned in their weapons; the holdouts also tried to steal the friendly Moros' cattle. As had happened in the Lake Lanao campaign, Pershing waited so long to attack that some natives questioned his sincerity and resolve. At last the two sides agreed that Pershing would withdraw and the Moros would then turn over their weapons. The general ordered his men off the field, but the Moros refused to honor their side of the bargain.

Pershing ordered his men back to Fort McKinley at

Zamboanga, then spread the word he would be taking a vacation with his family. Instead, he gathered a force of twelve hundred—some of them officers taken by surprise in their dress whites—and hurried back to Bud Bagsak without lights, part of the force traveling overland and others by boat along the shore. As he suspected, the Moros had left the *cotta* to tend to their crops and many of the women and children were away. Before they could call their families back, Pershing attacked. The morning of June 11, 1913, American artillery opened fire. The soldiers advanced through dense jungle, hacking their way through the trackless wilderness. Dressed in their finest clothes and prepared to die, the Moros counterattacked.

The battle continued until the morning of June 15. The Moros knew this was their last stand and, as Pershing wrote his wife, "The fighting was the fiercest I have ever seen." When artillerymen needed shorter-range ordinance, they cut the fuses off their canisters. When a new model of hand grenade proved disappointing, soldiers threw dynamite sticks in bundles of four instead. The Americans advanced to within a hundred yards of the main fortifications when the assault wavered and the soldiers started falling back. Dodging arrows and spears, General Pershing moved to the front of the line and ordered his officers to do likewise. The effect, Pershing's aide recalled later, was "electric." In the face of heavy fire, the Americans stormed the *cotta*'s bamboo fences and broke them down, taking the compound. The besieged Moros died to the last man. With this American victory, the last major organized resistance to Pershing's weapons law was crushed.

For his bravery in battle, General Pershing was nominated for the Medal of Honor. When he heard the news, he wrote the War Department asking them not to make the award. "I do not consider that my action on that occasion was such as to entitle me to be decorated with a Medal of Honor," he wrote. "I went to that part of the line because my presence there was needed."[7] The decorations board concurred and declined to make the award.

Pershing had left the Philippines before because he achieved his objectives and his health was declining. The same was true now. The general had secured the peace in Moro Province, at least for a while, and delivered a long list of successes. He was also physically spent by his tour in the tropics. During his four years in the big house at Zamboanga, Pershing had overseen the planning and construction of five hundred miles of roads, two hundred miles of telephone lines, thirty-seven medical stations, a tuberculosis treatment program, smallpox vaccinations, electric power plants, increases in trade and agriculture, and a more stable and fair legal system. He had set up a school for girls and made other inroads in the education system, though improvement there was limited by cultural differences. Most teachers in Moro Province were from the Catholic north, and the Moros resisted accepting them.

General Pershing felt ready for a change. He had done his duty well. He had been hospitalized for exhaustion and the lingering effects of malaria. He believed his condition might compromise his effectiveness as provincial governor. Besides, he and Frankie wanted their children to be educated in America. The two oldest had been in a kindergarten taught by the wife of an officer, and it was time for them to start school.

They and their brother, Warren, also had a new sister, Mary, born in the spring of 1912. Some time shortly after Mary's birth, the entire Pershing family was baptized in the American Episcopal Church by Bishop Charles Henry Brent. Bishop Brent was a Canadian-born missionary who had lived in the Philippines since 1901, declining several bishoprics in the United States to continue his ministry to the Filipinos, especially the Moros and other Muslims. Pershing's decision could have been the outward sign of a spiritual decision made long ago, or a mark of a new commitment to his faith. Having the whole family baptized may have been a way of calling for divine protection of the wife and children he loved so deeply. Whatever inner workings of the general's mind and heart that prompted the move, it was an important step of faith that they all took together.

In December 1913 the War Department ordered General John J. Pershing to command the Eighth Brigade at the Presidio, a fortified point overlooking the Golden Gate, the entrance to San Francisco Bay and one of the most strategically important installations on the West Coast. After a huge farewell party in Zamboanga, the family traveled to Manila to board their homebound ship.

They were at sea on Christmas Day, celebrating with a turkey dinner and presents for the children. Frankie was delighted at the prospect of making an American home for her family after four years away. They stopped for shore rest in Honolulu and then continued on to the United States, which three of the children scarcely remembered and the youngest had never seen, though they'd heard wonderful stories about it.

SEVEN

Beyond Understanding

S ENATOR W ARREN WAS so excited to see his grand-
children that he couldn't wait for them to come ashore. He
took an army tugboat into San Francisco Bay to meet their
ship and then climbed a rope ladder up the side and onto the
deck. The children swarmed over him as he greeted them and
their parents. On the tug with the senator were reporters and
photographers sent to cover the return of General Pershing,
hero of the battle against the Moros and a fast-rising brigadier.
They grouped the three girls and their brother for a portrait—
beautiful, blond-headed siblings born all around the world.
The oldest had been born in Japan, her two sisters in the
Philippines, and their brother in Wyoming.

At the Presidio, where he assumed command of the

Eighth Infantry Brigade on January 13, 1914, Pershing had his pick of quarters. He and Frankie chose a spacious house with a big yard facing the parade ground where the children would have plenty of room to play. The first few months in San Francisco were some of the happiest of the general's life. The weather was a delightful change from the tropics, the social scene was varied and interesting, and the children were in awe of their new American surroundings, especially the glories of the San Francisco zoo. Pershing took them to see the immensely popular Wild West Show of Buffalo Bill Cody, courtesy of complimentary tickets from Cody himself. Pershing and Cody had known each other more than twenty years earlier on the Western frontier.

The children were captivated by the spectacle and Pershing was pleasantly surprised to see Sioux scouts in the show whom he had commanded at Pine Ridge in the aftermath of the Wounded Knee massacre. "It reminded me of old times to see those Redskins on the mock warpath again," he wrote, "and the children sat in wonder at this and other thrilling performances. The kiddies were in ecstasy."[1]

The peaceful family interlude was short-lived. Mexico had been thrown into turmoil by the fall of longstanding dictator Porfirio Díaz and his exile to Paris. The country dissolved into anarchy and violence. Americans along the border braced for attacks by the bandits, insurgents, mercenaries, and vigilantes who ran wild in the northern Mexican *estados* (states), invading towns, ambushing trains, attacking isolated ranchers and travelers. Rebel leader Francisco "Pancho" Villa was rumored to be planning an invasion into U.S. territory. Pershing and the Eighth were ordered to Fort Bliss, near El Paso, Texas, to protect the American border.

Since the general and Frankie had no idea how long his posting would last, she decided to take the children to Cheyenne where Helen and Anne enrolled in school. Senator Warren had remarried while the Pershings were overseas, and everyone loved new Grandmother Clara, the former Clara Morgan, who was only a few years older than Frankie and shared her vivacious, unpretentious personality. Pershing went to visit them in Wyoming as often as his duties allowed.

In typical fashion, the general spent long hours drilling and inspecting his troops, though they saw no Mexican invaders. Pancho Villa did pay a courtesy call on the American commander and the two posed for a picture together. The Mexican leader, shorter and more heavyset than the general, was dressed in his Sunday best, his hair slicked back under his hat and a neat bow tie at his throat. The general stood beside him in high-collar uniform and campaign hat, smiling broadly.

Pershing took tea every afternoon at the Hotel Sheldon, where reporters gathered to swap stories and glean the latest tidbits. They considered the general a friendly, open, sociable officer, far more cordial than the haughty types they were used to dealing with at the fort.

He received a letter from his family almost every day, some of them including drawings by the children and pages covered with their arithmetic problems. Frankie loved bowling and often sent her latest scores. In the spring of 1915, Helen finished the third grade and Anne completed her first-grade year.

General and Mrs. Pershing had been apart fourteen months since they sailed home from the Philippines, and there was still no telling how long the unrest in Mexico would last. Pershing took leave to go to Cheyenne and escort his family back to the Presidio. He had decided to prepare quarters for them at Fort Bliss; they would join him in Texas soon. Before they left San Francisco, however, Frankie wanted the children to experience the excitement of the Panama-Pacific International Exposition. The exposition grounds were only a short distance from their house and Frankie had volunteered to help at the booth promoting Montessori education. This innovative learning method, developed in Italy by Dr. Maria Montessori, doubtless appealed to her because it replaced rigid conventional teaching styles with an approach that encouraged children to explore and learn in their own ways. Montessori students chose their own classroom activities and worked at a pace comfortable for them. Teachers taught indirectly by watching the children, guiding them, and making suggestions.

Frankie planned to join her husband shortly after the Wellesley West Coast alumnae meeting—a reception and banquet scheduled for August 25 in the Massachusetts Building on the exposition grounds. Invited to be one of the speakers, Frankie talked about how Wellesley prepared her for life by equipping her to handle new situations. Wellesley, she said, "has helped me in every kind of crisis, great or small, from the time they brought me and laid in my arms my first baby, to the time I backed out of an audience with the emperor of Japan in a train twelve yards long."[2]

The next night, August 26, Frankie and the children had a

houseful of company. Her dear friend Anne Orr Boswell, daughter Anne's namesake, and her two children were there for a visit. Mrs. Margaretta Gray Church, an old friend of Frankie's late mother who had happened upon her at the Montessori booth, was also spending the night. After the six children went to bed, the three ladies sat up talking until about midnight.

At two or three in the morning, Anne Boswell was awakened by a light coming from under her bedroom door. Opening it, she saw the hallway filled with smoke and flames roaring up the stairwell. She couldn't get to the bedrooms across the hall because of the smoke, and so climbed out her window. She walked along the roof to the room where her two sons, James and Philip, and the maid were asleep. She woke them by banging on the glass and pulled them out onto the roof with her, where they stood waiting for help. A noise woke Mrs. Church, who saw the smoke and fire in the hall and climbed out the window in the bathroom. Soldiers answering the fire bell caught Mrs. Church. Anne Boswell threw her boys, six and three, to soldiers before she and her maid jumped into the flowerbed.

Seeing a woman and young children safe, the firemen thought at first that the Pershings were all out of the house. When someone realized that neither James nor Philip was five-year-old Warren Pershing, a team of firefighters rushed inside as flames shot through the second-story roof and into the night sky. They found sisters Helen and Mary in one bedroom, and Frankie and little Anne in another—Anne's mother was sleeping with her because she had an upset stomach. All four were untouched by the fire—all four dead of smoke inhalation.

That left Warren. Private Fred Newscome went back in to look for him. Crawling on the floor under a thick layer of cinder-filled smoke, he found the boy in the upstairs hallway, unconscious but still breathing. Newscome carried him out the window and handed him down to other rescue workers, who rushed him to the hospital.

Investigators examining the charred shell of the house later reported that a glowing cinder of coal from the living room fireplace had rolled off the hearth and onto the newly varnished floor.

General Pershing heard the news from Norman Walker, an Associated Press correspondent in El Paso who saw an update to the story on the *El Paso Herald* Teletype. Walker called Pershing's office at Fort Bliss expecting to speak to his contact and friend, Pershing's aide Lieutenant James L. Collins. When a voice answered, Walker said he had more news on the Presidio fire. He assumed the general and his staff already knew about it.

"What fire?!" the voice demanded. It was Pershing on the line. Taken off guard, Walker read the Teletype dispatch. "Oh, God! My God! Read it again!" Pershing exclaimed. Walker reread the story and offered his condolences. The general said nothing at first, then asked, "Who is this?" Walker told him. "Thank you, Walker. It was very considerate of you to phone."[3]

Within the next day or so, Pershing received the last letter Frankie wrote him:

> The world is so clean this morning. There is the sound of meadow larks everywhere. And God be thanked for the sunshine and blue sky! Do you think there can be many people

in the world as happy as we are? I would like to live to be a thousand years old if I could spend all of that time with you.[4]

Helen Frances Pershing was thirty-five.

The general and Lieutenant Collins took the train west. Pershing cried the whole way, wailing, grieving a loss deeper than any words, a loss beyond understanding. At Bakersfield, California, they picked up Frank Helm, an old friend from Philippine days. Pershing put his arms around Helm's neck and held them there all the way to Oakland, weeping constantly. They crossed San Francisco Bay to the city. Pershing wanted to go straight to the funeral parlor, where four caskets waited. He asked to be left alone, then knelt and prayed before each casket in turn. Whatever spiritual assurance he had found in his baptism and the baptism of those now dead, whatever he felt of God's presence and his promise of eternal life and a peace beyond understanding, that was what he turned to for solace in this, the darkest, most hopeless moment of his life.

After nearly an hour he said he wanted to see the house. At the Presidio he looked over the blackened walls of the bedrooms and saw the doors between Warren's room and the smoke that had saved the boy's life. Warren had awakened before he was asphyxiated, then crawled into the hall where Private Newscome found him.

Pershing and his friends went from there to the hospital to pick up Warren. On their way to the hotel where they would stay for the time being, they passed the International Exposition grounds. When the general asked his son if he'd been there, he answered excitedly, "Oh yes! Mama takes us there often."[5] Pershing began trembling so hard he couldn't hold the boy and handed him to Helm.

Senator and Mrs. Warren arrived from Wyoming. The next day, the day Frankie and the children had planned to board the train for El Paso, the four coffins were loaded on the *Overland Limited* for Cheyenne and burial in the family plot. Beforehand there was an Episcopal service at the funeral parlor, which the general attended in dark civilian clothes. A hundred others squeezed inside while more waited on the sidewalk.

Pershing received an avalanche of condolence letters. Friends struggled to put into words how they had loved Frankie and the girls, and what joy they drew from the general's love for his family. The former president of Wellesley wrote of the wonderful speech Frankie had given at the alumnae reunion. "And in thirty-six hours that radiant spirit was gone, gone with her three little daughters."[6] Classmates from Helen and Anne's school wrote, as did Theodore Roosevelt, Mrs. Arthur MacArthur, the governor of Texas, the Japanese ambassador, Boy Scouts from the Philippines, senators, cabinet members, friends, admirers, and perfect strangers.

Warren Pershing went with his father back to Fort Bliss, where his spinster Aunt May moved in to help take care of him. Warren saw plenty of familiar faces in the Eighth Brigade, men who had served with his father in the Philippines. Still it was a temporary solution, since Pershing might be ordered into battle against Mexican insurgents any time. To give him a more permanent home, Warren went to live with Aunt May and her widowed sister, Aunt Elizabeth "Bess" Butler, who shared a house in Lincoln, Nebraska. He and his father sent a steady stream of letters back and forth. The general carefully saved his.

General Pershing instructed his sisters May and Bess to have a big birthday party for Warren, and to buy him a bicycle from his father. May reported the bike was a huge success. "O, he just jumped up and danced . . . I never saw a child so delighted . . . It is a Ray-Cycle and is considered first class in every way. It cost $22.50. He is not able to ride it alone yet but is learning."[7] Warren sent one of the party invitations he had typed himself in his thank-you letter to his father.

The general brooded over his decision to have the floors revarnished during renovation of the Presidio house. He thought the fire was his fault and obsessed over it in the aftermath of the tragedy. Yet as much as it was on his mind, Pershing never said a word about the fire to Warren then, or for the rest of his life.

General Pershing's ten-year marriage had transformed him, drawing out a depth of love, a sense of wonder, an appreciation of life he had never shown before. A notorious ladies' man became a doting and devoted husband and father. The deaths of Frances and their three daughters transformed him again. He would always miss them, always feel pain and longing at the thought of them. Though he kept deep and sincere relationships with his many old friends, new acquaintances had trouble breaking through his taciturn public persona. In time he would find romantic love again, but it was never the same. No one could ever take Frankie's place in his life or in his heart.

On June 14, 1917, the day after he arrived in Paris, Pershing visited Napoleon's tomb. Handed the emperor's sword, he declined it, saying he had not yet proven himself worthy to hold it.

Pershing with French commander-in-chief General Philippe Pétain. The two allies fought a harsh battle of words over "amalgamation," with Pétain insisting that American troops be assigned to French and British units and Pershing determined to maintain separate American brigades under American command.

After leading the Allied victory, Pershing was promoted to General of the Armies, the only American in history other than George Washington to hold such rank, and the only one to hold it during his lifetime.

A view of the welcoming celebration for returning soldiers. There had already been celebrations in New York and Philadelphia.

General Pershing riding in the parade welcoming returning soldiers to Washington, September 17, 1919.

General Pershing addresses a joint session of Congress, September 18, 1919.

EIGHT

Over There

M E X I C O H A D B E E N in turmoil since longtime dictator
Porfirio Díaz lost control of the country in 1911. After a series
of bloody internal battles, the rebel commander Venustiano
Carranza occupied Mexico City and was recognized by the
United States as the new Mexican leader. One of his former
allies, the rebel Pancho Villa, contested his claim and fought to
take power himself. After failing to defeat Carranza in the capital,
Villa moved north to rebuild his army and keep his hopes alive. In
retaliation against American support for Carranza, Villa attacked
Americans in the area. One notorious incident took place in the
Mexican state of Chihuahua, where Villa and his men ordered
sixteen American miners off a train, stripped them naked, and
shot them dead in cold blood.

This and other incidents infuriated the government in Washington and the American people. Their anger boiled over after Villa led four hundred of his henchmen onto U.S. soil before dawn on March 9, 1916, raiding the town of Columbus, New Mexico. They burned the buildings and killed eighteen residents, though the invaders suffered heavy losses of two hundred killed or wounded. President Woodrow Wilson knew the public would not allow such an attack to go unanswered. At the same time, he wanted to avoid war with Mexico at all cost.

Europe had been at war for more than a year and a half. In May 1915, when a German submarine torpedoed and sunk the British passenger liner *Lusitania*, 128 Americans lost their lives. In the months before the Columbus attack, the president made high-profile speeches supporting the Allies, and the Germans launched a massive assault on the French city of Verdun. America seemed to be inching closer to involvement in the fighting overseas. The last thing the country needed was to spark a war with its neighbor to the south.

The president had to have a military commander who was both a strong, resolute leader and a skilled, intuitive diplomat; an officer who could lead an invasion into Mexico without inciting the Mexicans to retaliate. The United States had legal cover for the move in a treaty allowing either side to chase "barbarians" into the other's territory, written with Indians in mind. Yet politically it was a very risky move. Based on his performance in Moro Province, General Pershing was Wilson's ideal man for the job.

The American invasion force assembled at Columbus. What had been a dusty desert settlement without electricity was transformed almost overnight into a vibrant tent city sporting hotels, gambling halls, bordellos, and even a newspaper. A squadron of canvas-covered Curtis biplanes flew in to provide reconnaissance and courier service. General Pershing prepared to join his troops, taking a small staff with him from Fort Bliss. Everyone who would be left behind clamored for a place in the action. One of the most relentless young officers begging Pershing to join the fight was Lieutenant George S. Patton Jr. Finally an exasperated Pershing snapped, "Everyone wants to go. Why should I favor you?"

"Because I want to go more than anyone else," Patton answered. Some days later Pershing decided to bring the lieutenant with him and called to ask when he could be ready.

"I'm already packed," Patton replied.[1]

Once again Pershing had been considering the idea of resigning from the army. Frankie's death had been such a terrible shock, and he was still affected by medical problems stemming from his years in Cuba and the Philippines. The Mexican campaign reinvigorated him and pushed aside all thoughts of retirement. Only a week after Villa's raid, on March 15, Pershing rode south out of Columbus at the head of a column of soldiers determined to capture or kill the invader.

Privately the general believed there was little chance they would find Villa in the vast Mexican desert. Nevertheless, he would put everything he and his command had into the effort. The first thirty-six hours they marched 140 miles. Horses and wagons sent up thick clouds of dust that soldiers endured by wearing goggles and bandanas. The thin atmosphere and cloudless sky brought scorching daytime temperatures of 115 degrees and nights near freezing.

Once when the general was with a small detachment separated from the rest of the force, they were surrounded by two hundred ragtag Mexican soldiers led by one of Villa's former allies. Pershing calmly told their commander what he was doing and why, had a cordial conversation with him, and got safe passage to continue—though they shot at Pershing's men later on. In other action, Lieutenant Patton led a squad of ten men who killed two Mexican leaders including Julio Cárdenas, commander of Villa's personal bodyguard. Patton delivered the bodies to Pershing's headquarters lashed to a car fender like deer, which brought him wide renown in the American press.

As they entered the poor villages of the Mexican interior, Pershing ordered his men to treat the people with respect and to buy their goods at fair prices. As with the Moros in years past, Mexican villagers were surprised and pleased that the Americans treated them not as enemies but as friends. The general led his force five hundred miles into Mexico with no sign of their quarry. He and the commanders in Washington worried about his long supply lines through the desert. He had far outrun his telephone and telegraph communications and was now sending dispatches by airplane north to the end of the wire. The longer they stayed and the farther they went, the more they raised Mexican suspicions. Fearing Carranza's forces might surround them and cut them off, the U.S. government stationed more troops along the Mexican border and nationalized the National Guard in nearby states, giving them 150,000 men in all.

Neither country wanted the fight to escalate. Pershing settled his men in the town of Colonia Dublan near the U.S. border, where they waited six months for negotiators to reach an agreement on American withdrawal. In September Pershing was promoted to major general, adding a second star to his rank. As Christmas approached, he wrote to his sister May, asking her to buy gifts and send cards to family and friends for him. To help sustain the morale of his troops during their long wait, the general staged a magnificent Christmas party in Colonia Dublan with a sixty-five-foot tree made out of dozens of small trees. It was covered with electric lights and topped by an American flag. A men's chorus of four hundred sang patriotic songs and the troops enjoyed a lavish Christmas dinner.

The Mexican incursion ended when Pershing led his men back across the border and into Columbus on February 5, 1917. They never saw Pancho Villa or any sign of him. The notorious rebel eluded capture and remained at large until he was shot and killed six years later. Though it failed to achieve its military objective, the exercise was valuable preparation for the all-out war Pershing and the American army would join in only a few months.

Pershing's command was the largest in the nation since the Civil War. It underscored the value of modern tools of warfare such as motorized trucks, aerial photography, and radios—and trained soldiers to use them. It pointed out glaring deficiencies in America's military recruiting and supply systems. It further reinforced to Pershing the key importance of planning, communication, and attention to detail. Nourishing food and competent medical care were as important as ammunition. Befriending the locals was an easy way to make valuable allies. At the end of the Mexican campaign, General Pershing headed arguably the best-trained, best-disciplined, best-prepared American military force in a generation.

The general's next assignment was to command the Southern Department, headquartered at Fort Sam Houston near San Antonio, Texas. Before he took up that post, he went to California to visit Lieutenant Patton and his family. The extended Patton clan had amassed fortunes in California real estate and textiles, reportedly making the lieutenant—owner of polo ponies and a yacht—the wealthiest officer in the army. Pershing had met Patton's sister Anne Wilson Patton, two years younger than her brother and known as "Nita," when she came to visit Patton and his wife at Fort Bliss.

Nita, twenty-nine, was tall, athletic, blonde, and beautiful, with striking Nordic features. She was attracted to the dashing general and the feeling was mutual. Some in the family thought he would ask for her hand in marriage before he left for San Antonio. Nita's father thought Pershing was too socially inferior, though her sister-in-law, Patton's wife Beatrice, encouraged the match. She had her daughters send letters to the general in Mexico, which filled his eyes with tears as they reminded him of his own girls. Nita wrote him then, too, and sent a letter of congratulations on his promotion. When Beatrice asked the general if he thought it would be good for Nita if she married him, he answered, "Yes, I do."[2]

When Nita visited her brother and the general later in Texas, Pershing wrote to his sister in Nebraska:

May, do you remember Miss Patton? She is here for a few days. Well, May dear, she is the finest and best woman. I had thought I could never love, but she has made a place all her own. I am telling you all this, May, you and [Bess], *very confidentially*. So please do not mention it to a single soul in the world. I have been so broken-hearted and bereft. It will make a home for little Warren.[3]

By April 1917, General Pershing's plans for the future were overshadowed by events in Europe. On February 1 of that year, while the general was still camped at Colonia Dublan, Germany resumed unrestricted submarine attacks in the Atlantic, which they had suspended the year before at President Wilson's insistence. On February 24, less than three weeks after Pershing returned from Mexico, British intelligence revealed that Germany had been trying to convince Mexico to declare war against the United States.

The German foreign secretary, Arthur Zimmermann, wired a coded telegram to Johann von Bernstorff, German ambassador to the United States in Washington, on January 16. Three days later, as requested by Zimmermann, von Bernstorff forwarded the message—sent originally as seemingly random groups of numbers—to the German ambassador in Mexico, Heinrich von Eckardt. Germany anticipated strong objection from America to the resumption of unrestricted submarine warfare scheduled for February 1. The instructions to von Eckardt were that if the United States seemed about to declare war on Germany, he should ask the Mexicans for an alliance. In exchange, the

Germans would help Mexico reclaim Texas, New Mexico, and Arizona from the United States.

On March 1, the Zimmermann telegram was published in American newspapers, sparking public outrage. On March 15, Czar Nicholas II abdicated the Russian throne, freeing German soldiers on the Eastern front to join the assault against France. Four days after President Wilson requested it, the U.S. House of Representatives declared war against Germany on April 6.

With its congressional vote to join the fight, the United States entered a war that had started almost three years before. It began with the unraveling of an interconnected series of bilateral treaties negotiated over nearly a century in hopes of maintaining peace in Europe. Though these treaties were largely successful, ethnic, political, and religious skirmishes came and went over the years. One direct antecedent of the Great War took place in October 1908, when the central European monarchy of Austria-Hungary formally annexed Bosnia and Herzegovina. This was an affront to the Russian Empire and its satellite nation of Serbia: to the Russians because they feared it weakened their standing in Europe, and to the Serbs because there were kindred ethnic Slavs in the annexed territory.

The matter simmered there through a pair of regional conflicts known as the Balkan Wars, until June 28, 1914. On that day in the Bosnian city of Sarajevo, Gavrilo Princip, a radical Bosnian student, shot and killed the heir to the throne of Austria-Hungary, Archduke Franz Ferdinand, and his wife, Sophie, Duchess of Hohenberg. As Austria-Hungary considered how to retaliate, Serbia interceded on Bosnia's behalf. To keep Serbia out of the argument, Austria-Hungary delivered a series of ultimatums, knowing the Serbians would never accept them all. When Serbia balked, Austria-Hungary declared war.

The next day, July 29, Russia mobilized against Austria-Hungary in support of Serbia. Germany declared war on Russia in support of Austria-Hungary. Within days France and the United Kingdom declared war on Germany over the neutrality of Belgium and control of Alsace-Lorraine, annexed by Germany from France in 1871. The German army came roaring into France, bound for Paris. With British help, the French stopped the advance but could not mount an effective counterattack. Long-range rifles and artillery, fighter planes, poison gas, tanks, and other modern weapons made it impossible for one side to advance against the other. Weapons reached too far and caused too much destruction for traditional infantry and cavalry advances to be effective.

This had been evident during the Russo-Japanese war, where some of these modern weapons were deployed on a large scale for the first time. But for all the observers who saw the result, none of them evidently learned that new weapons required new tactics. They still thought in terms of the Civil War era or the Franco-Prussian war, when the pace of battle and the reach of an advance were determined by the pace of a horse, the length of a saber, and the range of a black powder cartridge.

Both sides dug protective trenches in order to withstand enemy bombardment, and there they waited, firing and taking fire month after month, season after season. During three years of conflict in France before America declared war, the combatants had already suffered ten million casualties—700,000 in the Battle of Verdun alone—spread along six thousand miserable, muddy, disease-infested miles of trenches. Some battle lines had scarcely moved in years, with each yard gained at the cost of thousands of young lives. One British offensive advanced two miles at a cost of 620,000 casualties, 50,000 of them in a single day. French general Robert Nivelle boasted he would march through the German lines in forty-eight hours, then he advanced into a blizzard of machine-gun fire that crushed his attack with the loss of 200,000 men. Another French assault gained five hundred yards with 250,000 lost.

General Pershing had no idea what assignment the War Department might offer him. All he knew was that he could not bear to wait out the American offensive behind a desk. The day Congress declared war, he wrote to President Wilson and to Secretary of War Newton Baker requesting assignment. He may have had some encouragement from a telegram his father-in-law sent, saying, "Wire me today whether and how much French you speak, read, and write."[4] Rusty though he was, Pershing answered that he was fluent. He also received a telegram from General Hugh Scott, the army chief of staff, ordering him to select four infantry regiments and one of artillery to command overseas.

On May 10 Pershing arrived in Washington to meet with Scott and the secretary of war. Newton D. Baker was a short, bespectacled, slightly built and mild-mannered lawyer, who two years earlier had been mayor of Cleveland, Ohio. Despite being a dedicated pacifist himself—he declined to lead Boy Scouts because he thought the organization was too militaristic—Baker soon proved to be an effective member of the war cabinet and a strong Pershing ally. One of his first key decisions was who would lead the American Expeditionary Force that the United States would assemble to fight in France. There were several likely candidates, including General Scott and Pershing's old commander General Wood.

On paper Wood, a physician and Medal of Honor recipient, seemed the likely candidate. He was the most senior general in the army, a previous chief of staff idolized by his subordinates, and friends with many important politicians and businessmen. Unfortunately for him and his supporters, he was also notoriously indiscreet, politically ambitious, and suffered pain from a recurring brain tumor for which he had had two operations already; a third after the war would kill him. Also, notwithstanding his long years of service, he had never commanded a large force in the field.

Baker met with Pershing and liked him. Both men placed a high value on careful planning and decisive action. After thinking it over, the secretary called the general to a second meeting to tell him he would lead the AEF. Baker's philosophy, he wrote later, was to "select a commander in whom you have confidence; give him power and responsibility, and then work your head off to give him everything he needs and support him in every decision he makes."[5] He told General Pershing he would give him two orders in his new position: to go to Europe and to come home. The rest was up to him.

At first Baker and President Wilson planned to send Pershing overseas at the head of a division cobbled together from whatever forces they could collect on short notice. Two days later Baker told Pershing that plans had been changed and he would leave for Europe as soon as possible with a core staff. His divisions would be sent to France as soon as they could be trained and equipped.

Many who had served with Pershing over the years begged to go with him, General Scott among them. Pershing had great respect for these officers, some with service records stretching back to the Little Big Horn more than forty years before. For all their patriotism and eagerness, these men were too old for the job. Pershing told them so gently but firmly. One member of his inner circle making the trip was George Patton, whom Pershing promoted to captain. Patton's family, including his sister Nita, came east to see him off. Some of Pershing's friends were convinced he and Nita would announce their engagement before the troops sailed; Nita evidently thought so too.

As Pershing plunged himself into preparation for leading an army thousands of miles from home, he focused on several essential areas. First, he would have to build and train his staff himself; there was no standing cadre of officers who could take on the necessary responsibilities. Second, he would resist intense lobbying by the French and British to use American soldiers merely to fill in their ranks; his men would only serve as American units under American officers, especially considering the bloody futility of much of the fighting. The British had already asked for five hundred thousand recruits to train and command. Pershing would have none of it. Third, he would have to make up for decades of atrophy in America's standing regular army; the country was woefully unprepared to fight any sort of major war, much less their first conflict with modern weapons on the other side of an Atlantic bristling with belligerent German submarines.

President Wilson was a major contributor to the U.S. lack of preparedness. Hearing that the army staff was working up plans for war with Germany in 1916, he angrily ordered the planning stopped and every officer involved transferred out of Washington. America declared war without the men or infrastructure to wage it, even though the war in Europe had been going on for years. The Allies had hoped America would send forty-five hundred airplanes to the battlefield. In 1917 the United States had a total of fifty-five warplanes, none battle-ready, and thirty-five army air officers who knew how to fly them.

Pershing and his staff of about two hundred left New York on May 28, 1917. Nita Patton was by the general's side on the pier. Their appearance fanned rumors they were going to be married, if not before the war, then as soon as possible afterward. In pouring rain and unseasonably cold wind, the soldiers boarded a tug for transfer to the SS *Baltic*, a large, two-funnel Atlantic liner of the White Star Line. Pershing had a spacious suite and his chief of staff, Major James Harbord, occupied the cabin next door. The general expected to spend his time during the crossing completing a detailed action plan that they would implement as soon as they landed. He also scheduled French lessons twice a day for every soldier on board.

The ship sailed with its portholes and windows papered over in order not to show its lights to the German U-boats. As the vessel passed Nantucket into open sea lanes, it picked up an escort of two American destroyers. The soldiers wore civilian clothes so that if they were sunk, the Germans wouldn't shoot at them in the lifeboats. Pershing and Harbord huddled to discuss recruiting, French railroad capacity, and countless other details. He believed he would need a million men for the job: that meant a million uniforms, two million shoes, and three million meals a day. The final number was actually about twice that.

As the *Baltic* approached British waters, the destroyers peeled off. The ship docked at Liverpool, then the main Atlantic passenger terminal, on June 8, welcomed by the lord mayor of the city, senior British military officers, and an honor guard of Royal Welsh Fusiliers. Pershing reviewed the troops, ramrod straight and immaculate as always, outfitted in gloves and dress sword. The British press and the crowd at the pier were impressed.

The king sent the royal train to take the Americans to Euston Station in London, where they would attend a round of social events Pershing found unavoidable, even though they robbed him of time for the briefings and fact-gathering he knew was essential. The first order of business the next morning was an audience with King George V, who warmly welcomed the general, and whom Pershing liked. The king showed Pershing a statue of Queen Victoria not far from a spot the Germans had bombed. "The g-- d--- Kaiser even tried to blow up his own grandmother!"[6] the monarch fumed. She was Czar Nicholas's grandmother too.

Almost immediately his hosts warned Pershing that the way forward was for Americans to send them recruits to replenish their lines decimated by three years of war and millions of casualties. The term used was "amalgamation." True to form, General Pershing had planned ahead. He carried his orders from President Wilson, which directed him "to cooperate with the forces of other countries employed against the enemy; but in doing so the underlying idea must be kept in view that the forces of the United States are a separate and distinct component of the combined forces, the identity of which must be preserved." The order continued, "This fundamental rule is subject to such minor exceptions in particular circumstances as your judgment may approve . . . You will exercise full discretion in determining the manner of cooperation."[7]

Pershing saw the scale of challenges ahead of him from a new perspective when he asked how many British ships would be available to carry American soldiers to France. The Chief of the Imperial General Staff, General William Robertson, said there were none. Meeting with British prime minister David Lloyd George the next day, Pershing learned how badly the German torpedoes had crippled the Allied merchant fleet. In April alone, the British had lost one and a half million tons of shipping, only a fraction of which had been replaced.

Pershing sailed for France after less than a week in London, landing at the port of Boulogne on the morning of June 13. His train arrived in Paris at six-thirty that evening, timed by the French government for when workers would be on their way home and could see and welcome the Americans who had come to save them. They were in desperate need. Seven corps of soldiers, upward of two hundred thousand men, frustrated and demoralized by General Nivelle's arrogant incompetence, had recently laid down their arms and refused to fight. The Germans were closing in.

Pershing felt the desperation of the thousands who jammed the rail platform at the Gare du Nord. The crowd broke down the gates, showered him with flowers, and waved a sea of tiny American flags. His car crawled forward, surrounded by cheering factory workers, storekeepers, and shop girls. Children climbed trees to see and wave; some of their parents and grandparents wept. Creeping along the wide Parisian boulevards, he came finally to the Place de la Concorde, near the American Embassy, and to a lavish suite at the Hôtel de Crillon. When he reappeared on a balcony outside his room, a new cheer surged from the people waiting below.

The next day Pershing visited Napoleon's tomb and was presented with the former emperor's sword, which he kissed respectfully but did not take in his hands. He felt he had not yet proven himself worthy to hold it. "Magnificent!" said a French officer nearby. The general went to lay a wreath at the tomb of the Marquis de Lafayette, who as a young man had fought bravely and been wounded in the American War of Independence. Colonel Charles F. Stanton accompanied Pershing to the cemetery. Inspired by the moment, Colonel Stanton spoke for all Americans when he declared, "Lafayette, we are here!"[8]

NINE

Making Ready

ON JUNE 16, 1917, Pershing met for the first time with the commander-in-chief of the French army, General Philippe Pétain. The French general, half a head shorter than Pershing and sporting a bushy gray handlebar mustache, had a face only lightly lined by his years of service. Like his American counterpart, Pétain had advanced rapidly in rank after a long career in the army. A colonel at fifty-eight, he had bought a house and planned to retire in the spring of 1914. After the war began, he became chief of staff in three years.

In April 1917 legions of soldiers staged a passive mutiny, refusing to fight under General Robert Nivelle after his disastrous offensive at the River Aisne, where a poorly planned attack cost the French 271,000 casualties in twelve days. Pétain replaced

Nivelle, restored the troops' trust, and improved the quality of their food and medical care. Long experience had taught him, as it had Pershing, the value of planning and attention to detail. France hailed Pétain as a national hero for reviving the army and giving the nation new hope. Still, Pétain knew, the country's independence hung by a thread. His army could not hold off the German juggernaut much longer. Pershing and his shiploads of fresh fighters were France's last hope.

In their meeting, Pershing realized for the first time how desperate the French were. Pétain explained that he could no longer mount any large-scale offensive. All his army could do was try to defend their positions and wait for the Americans. "I hope it is not too late," he said somberly.[1] French and British generals and politicians still thought they could persuade the Americans to send an army of infantrymen and machine gunners to fill out their ranks. They insisted there was no time for Americans to train and transport their own fighting units, officer corps, and support systems. French and British regiments were already formed, already on the front. All they needed was more men on the line.

Pershing held his ground. He had seen the disastrous effects of Allied strategy and their largely defensive posture. Americans would not fight a defensive war. It wasn't the American way. They were there not to hold the line as the Allies had done for years but to take the offensive and sweep the field.

The Allies doubted the American ability to form their army rapidly enough to save France. The United States had no large standing military force. Where would the men come from? And where were the American officers to lead them? From the

European perspective, Americans were unproven on the battle-field against first-tier opposition. Their only experience in more than fifty years had been against Indians, half-hearted colonials, jungle savages, and tin pot dictators. How could they hope to defeat one of the most powerful armies in the history of the world?

Even King George came to call, trying to persuade Pershing to turn American soldiers over to standing armies already in the field. A month after he landed in France, Pershing released a statement declaring, "The United States will put its troops on the battlefront when it shall have formed an army worthy of the American people."[2]

One of Pershing's first decisions was where to land his troops and where they would live until enough soldiers were in place to execute an effective attack. The most obvious landing sites were the ports along the English Channel, with their bustling docks, warehouses, and ready access by rail. The problem was that the English jealously guarded their role as protector of the channel ports. If the Germans attacked there, the king and his advisers would pressure Pershing again to turn his men over to them. Or they might balk at cooperating with American commanders. Either way, political issues would affect military efficiency. Also those ports were already choked with men and supplies moving back and forth between England and France.

Farther west along the coast was the huge port of Le Havre at the mouth of the Seine, gateway to Paris. The French guarded this region on their own and would bristle at the implication that they couldn't protect their own capital, though Pershing and Pétain both surely knew they could not.

Pershing decided to base his operation in the Pays de la Loire region, farther south on the Atlantic coast, with its three deep-water ports, St. Nazaire, La Pallice, and Bassens. There was rail service from there to Paris, the ports were relatively quiet and unaffected by the war, and it was only forty miles from a major German supply line Pershing was eager to disrupt.

General Pershing moved out of the opulent Hôtel de Crillon into an equally luxurious house in town loaned by Ogden Mills, a California multimillionaire who owned a racing stable in France. The Crillon was a historic place as well as a beautiful one: in its gilded salon Benjamin Franklin had signed the treaty with France recognizing the newly independent United States. Pershing told a friend, however, that if he were paying his bill it would take ten years to settle the account; the Crillon was one of the most expensive hotels in one of the most expensive cities in Europe.

On June 26 the first wave of American troops, fourteen thousand men of the First Division, docked at St. Nazaire. Then and later, General Pershing seemed unimpressed with the military bearing and overall performance of his recruits. At West Point, Pershing got the silent treatment from cadets who saw only the stern disciplinarian and never the jovial partygoer. In France, the personal isolation between Pershing and his men was magnified a thousandfold. Of necessity only a few soldiers who served under him ever saw the person behind the general's stars—there would be four of them as of October, with his brevet promotion skipping him over lieutenant general to full general. Therefore, as hundreds of cadets had resented and despised Pershing for his seemingly insufferable nit-picking, hundreds of thousands of soldiers in France soon felt the same way.

The general appeared to be everywhere at once, inspecting everything and unhappy with all of it. Enlisted men and junior officers who had been civilians weeks before withstood a torrent of criticism. Uniforms were to be clean and properly worn in all weather and in spite of the mud. Living quarters had to be spotless, shoes shined, rifles oiled and ready, rows of marching men straight, horses well groomed and properly shod, kitchen garbage emptied promptly. He inspected construction offices, mail facilities, bakeries, hospitals, telephone exchanges, and the office of graves registration. If a soldier turned his head in formation to look at the general, he was ordered out of line to stand at attention with eyes forward for half an hour. As reporter Heywood Broun observed, "They will never call him 'Papa' Pershing."[3]

Writing of the general then, James Harbord, by now a colonel and Pershing's chief of staff, observed:

> He thinks very clearly and directly . . . He can talk to people straighter when calling them down than anyone I have ever seen. He has a naturally good disposition and a keen sense of humor. He loses his temper occasionally, and stupidity and vagueness irritate him more than anything else . . . He develops a great fondness for people he likes and is indulgent toward their faults, but at the same time is relentless when convinced of inefficiency. Personal loyalty to friends is strong in him, but does not blind him to the truth.[4]

Pershing had to get out of Paris. Social invitations poured in, as did drop-in visitors who kept him from his work. On September 6 the general transferred AEF headquarters to Chaumont, 150 miles to the southeast. There the Americans occupied a quadrangle of four-story barracks with red tile roofs. Pershing's office was on the second floor, furnished with only the most basic necessities. He lived five miles away in the Château Val des Écoliers, an elegant stone mansion with a high pitched roof and elaborately carved dormers. The general traveled in a Locomobile limousine, a large, expensive, but severe looking American car equipped with double rear wheels to negotiate the ever-present mud.

General Pershing was always on the lookout for capable leaders and staff officers, and he was often disappointed by men he considered inefficient, weak, duplicitous, lazy, or unimaginative. Even officers with many years of service failed to meet Pershing's standards. Few of them had had any chance to lead large forces in the field. Many had little understanding of the art of war in the twentieth century.

Most of all Pershing wanted intelligent, observant officers who could identify problems accurately and solve them swiftly no matter what. In October, Pershing went to a demonstration of a new attack method by Major Theodore Roosevelt Jr., son of the former president. Afterward he asked the division commander to critique what they had seen. When the commander stumbled, Pershing lashed out at him in front of his men and then gave the same treatment to another officer who tried to respond. A captain in the division, George Marshall, touched the general's arm as he turned to leave and said, "General Pershing, there is something to be said here and I think I should say it."

As other officers looked on aghast, Captain Marshall challenged

Pershing's harsh assessment and held his ground under the general's rapid-fire questioning. As American troop strength in France grew, Pershing later promoted Marshall to operations officer of the First Army. A generation afterward, Marshall would become army chief of staff, secretary of state, and mastermind of the plan to rebuild Europe in the wake of the Second World War. All his life he would attribute his success, in part, to Pershing's example.

Another soldier who impressed General Pershing was a sentry, a buck private who halted the commander's massive Locomobile at a muddy checkpoint during a fierce downpour. Pershing's orderly got out of the limousine and told the sentry General Pershing was inside. The sentry saluted and said his orders were that every passenger must get out of every vehicle and be identified. The general's military aide got out next and explained the situation; still the sentry held firm. The orderly got out again and warned the sentry he was about to get into big trouble for making the general step out in the rain and mud.

"Don't you realize who this is?" the orderly exclaimed. "General Pershing!"

Profanely and emphatically the private declared that it didn't matter who was in the car. There would be no exceptions. "Those are my orders," he said without apology.

Hearing this, Pershing got out of the car, his mirror-shined boots and perfectly creased trousers sinking in mud past the bottom of his overcoat. The sentry saluted and said, "I am sorry that I had to make you get out of the car in all this mud and rain, but those were my orders."

The next day Pershing had him promoted to sergeant.[5]

Pershing continued to be equally definitive in dealing with people who failed to measure up to his expectations. Among the senior generals he evaluated for Secretary of War Baker, Pershing advised that one of them was "very well informed on military history, but has very little experience in recent years in handling troops." Another was old for his years and Pershing warned: "We want only strong, active men, and cannot afford to take chances on weaklings or others who have stood still." Bringing a third into the field would "simply be a waste of time, with no result except failure."

General J. Franklin Bell, Medal of Honor recipient and former chief of staff, had pestered Pershing for a war command literally until he boarded the *Baltic* in New York Harbor. Still insistent, he came to France to ask again in person. "No officer has inspired me with a more sincere opinion of personal character and worth than you," Pershing wrote in a letter. Even so, "Frankly, General, I do not think you can stand the work and I beg of you to accept this as final . . . My personal advice to you, if I were not in command, would be exactly to the same effect."[6]

As the war effort grew, Pershing struggled to find a senior officer who could take charge of the mammoth supply and support network being built. One of the candidates he tried out in the position was General Richard Blatchford, an old friend who had served with him in Mexico. It was soon clear that Blatchford was not up to the job and Pershing relieved him. Blatchford was angry at what he saw as a personal betrayal and a blot on his long record of service. Eventually he complained to the secretary of war, prompting a blunt letter from Pershing. He had tried to let his friend down easy, saying he was needed Stateside. Now that he'd been pushed, Pershing told the unvarnished truth:

> I have refrained from going into this because of my almost lifelong friendship for you and my reluctance to say anything that might be disagreeable. The truth is, however, that in the position in which you were assigned your services were not satisfactory and did not warrant your retention on the very important duty involved . . . It might have been better to have advised you at the time.[7]

Drawing on his observations and experience in Cuba, the Philippines, and Mexico, Pershing insisted on creating logistics and supply systems to support a winning army, before committing that army to the field. The French and British complained louder than ever that Pershing had to get into the fight one way or the other, whether combined with them or in separate American divisions. Pershing would fight when he was ready.

A full-strength American army would need forty-five thousand tons of supplies a day. There was no way to ferry that volume of goods from the United States or even from England, the general decided. He had to develop a network for purchasing as much as possible from local sources. Pershing devised a three-tiered supply network: eight base depots across the theater with forty-five days of supplies each, intermediate depots closer to the action with thirty days' stores, and numerous smaller advance bases near the battlefronts with fifteen days' worth of goods.

Essential as the supply function was, Pershing still had to lead an army in battle. He needed a trusted right arm to run the support network so he could concentrate on fighting a war. After his first two choices failed to perform, Secretary Baker wanted to send a general from Washington as co-commander. Pershing objected, insisting that only one person could be on top of the chain of command or else confusion and disorganization would doom the entire effort. This was the military principle of unity of command and inviolable in Pershing's eyes. Baker accepted Pershing's argument, though Pershing knew that his third pick had to meet the standard or Washington would step in again.

This time Pershing chose his former chief of staff, now General Harbord, commanding the Second Division. Harbord had hoped to be promoted to corps commander and was disappointed at the thought of being taken off the battlefield. Yet out of loyalty to Pershing, Harbord said he didn't even need to sleep on it, but would accept the assignment immediately.

Almost overnight, nagging and seemingly insurmountable problems were identified and solved. Harbord was a master at his task. He had a special train outfitted with sleeping quarters, kitchen, telegraph and telephone, and two automobiles. He scoured the supply chain looking for inefficiencies, bottlenecks, and poor performance. He also changed the way he appealed to his workforce.

Pershing had promised dock workers a place in the trenches if they worked hard. Harbord sent the hardest workers on leave to the Riviera and promised them room on the first ships home after the war. He had ports compete to see who could unload the

most cargo and published the winners' names in military newspapers and in their hometown press. The AEF inspector general
reported, "In the twinkling of an eye . . . it was as if some great
force had suddenly awakened from a slumber."[8]

One of Pershing's most invaluable staff members, and one
of the very few whose friendship trumped military decorum,
was Charlie Dawes. The old friend and struggling lawyer from
University of Nebraska days was now a wealthy and successful
banker, investor, and politician. He had been appointed comp-
troller of the currency under President McKinley and was an
early visionary in the new business of municipal power generation. Dawes volunteered for the army engineering corps, though
his engineering experience consisted of a summer job holding a
surveyor's string. Arriving in Paris, he was a welcome visitor at
Pershing's lavish Paris mansion and then followed the general to
Chaumont.

Pershing appointed his friend chief of purchasing for the
AEF. Dawes was delighted at the chance to serve and went immediately to work on a serious and longstanding problem. The
Americans scrambled constantly to find enough coal. They had
to compete with the French and British for supplies. Rail cars
were unavailable. Washington seemed to deliver only red tape.
Through tenacity, analytical ability, and organizational skill,
Dawes knocked down impediments one by one: he found sources
of coal in Britain, rail cars on both sides of the English Channel,
and cargo space on cross-channel vessels. These were the first of
many problems Charlie Dawes solved with remarkable efficiency.

For taking such a load off his shoulders, Pershing forgave

Charlie for breaches of military decorum no one else could have survived unscathed. He was the only soldier in the AEF who called the ranking general "Jack" in public. During one memorable staff meeting, everyone in the room rose when General Pershing entered the room, except for Dawes, who stayed seated with a cigar in his mouth. The other officers stared at him in disbelief, then looked at the general for his reaction. "Charlie," the general said, "when the commanding general walks into the room it is customary to move your cigar from one side of your mouth to the other."[9] When they had an important meeting to attend, Pershing sent his orderly to Dawes's quarters to help him get his uniform on correctly.

With all his public duties there was also a private matter on Pershing's mind: his pending engagement to Nita Patton. They had parted evidently as lovers. She wrote him from California:

> It was a Sunday evening when we kissed goodbye. So many weeks have gone since then. All kinds of things have happened. For you many wonderful things, experiences that have marked epochs in the world's history. But in it all our love has lain warm in our hearts. Just think if you had gone away before you asked me if I loved you. Unspoken love is such a feeble thing, a prey to so many doubts and fears. I thank God that He let us have those unforgettable weeks, that we could see each other and kiss away each other's tears before we parted.[10]

When her brother heard she was planning to visit General Pershing in France, Patton though it was a bad idea. Officers' wives weren't permitted in France, and Nita coming to be with the commanding general would look very improper. He was also afraid his sister would send along a newspaper clipping with gossip that she was about to marry the head of the AEF.

Patton need not have worried about his sister. Pershing had written her less and less, and she was getting impatient with him. "Darlingest John," she wrote, "I think I'll divorce you if you don't write soon. Just now I want you, right here, I want you to hear you say, 'I love you.' I am a lovesick maiden, and I am lonesome." [11]

Later Nita would be describing Darlingest John to others as a "little tin god on wheels." At that point Pershing could not have cared less. Still handsome at fifty-seven, he had found new companionship closer at hand.

Into the Fight

LOUISE CROMWELL BROOKS was twenty-seven and beautiful. She was also married and the stepdaughter of a financier worth $150 million, equal to a multi-billion-dollar fortune today. Her porcelain skin and aristocratic features turned faces in the drawing rooms of Washington DC and in Paris where she had a second home. She was part of the Parisian social circle that embraced the commander of the AEF. General Pershing had been an unabashed ladies' man in his younger years, then remade himself as a faithful and devoted husband as long as he was married. Single again, he enjoyed the company and attentions of the opposite sex once more. Women of all ages were drawn to his good looks, charm, intelligence, and ability on the dance floor; they were, of course, also impressed by his power and position.

The general and Mrs. Brooks first met at one of the parties, receptions, or dinners Pershing was constantly invited to and felt compelled to sometimes attend. They were attracted to each other immediately. Brooks was a sensuous, adventuresome woman always on the prowl for sexual adventure. Pershing, though thirty years older, found in Louise the emotional and physical fulfillment Nita Patton could never supply from far-off California. However he felt about Nita, those feelings were swamped by his infatuation for Louise. They may have begun an affair, though the evidence is inconclusive. In fact, details of the relationship are obscured to the extent that some historians believe the two first met at the end of Pershing's tour in Europe.

According to Pershing biographer Gene Smith, Louise suggested she and the general marry. Pershing knew better than to think she would ever settle down. "Louise," he supposedly told her, "marrying you would be like buying a book for somebody else to read."[1] Louise eventually married a soldier, but not General Pershing. After the war, she divorced her husband in Paris and wed Douglas MacArthur. They divorced after seven years and she was divorced twice more. She then went on to other affairs. Meanwhile, Pershing turned his attention to the woman who would be the great love of the rest of his life.

At a Paris reception in June 1917, Pershing met a young painter who was already making a name for herself in the city's artistic circles. Micheline Resco was far down the scale in wealth and social status compared with Louise Brooks. But she was her equal and more in natural beauty and feminine charm. Petite, blonde, and blue-eyed, Micheline was a naturalized French citizen born in Romania. Her sparkling disposition and ready laugh sometimes made her seem even younger than her twenty-three years. She was in Paris to paint, and she arranged to do Pershing's portrait.

He sat for the portrait, a sketch in left three-quarter profile, his features sharp and trim, the shoulders and uniform jacket rendered in a few quick impressionist strokes. Soon, painter and subject were lovers. Ever since Frankie's death, Pershing had missed having someone he could confide in completely, around whom he could fully let go of the burdens of command. With Frankie he had been able to set aside his strict military manner and let the deep, tender emotions within him well up to the surface. He did this to some extent with his closest friends—Charlie Dawes in particular—but the refuge he found in his time alone with Frankie was on an entirely different level. The pressures of war and the isolation of command doubtless intensified the general's need to find a place to let loose his feelings.

He found what he needed in Micheline. When they first met, it was hard for them to communicate since her English was even more limited than his French. They began spending more time together. According to his official diary, whenever he was in Paris, the general regularly went for a portrait sitting or an evening French lesson. Pershing's position made it impossible for him to hide an affair from his personal staff, and he didn't even try. He sent notes to Micheline by junior officers arranging times for their liaisons. When he went to see her, he had the military insignia removed from his car and rode up front beside the driver. Other times he would send his car and driver for her.

Another great emotional anchor for him was his son, Warren, his closest remaining link with Frankie. He still thought about her, dreamed about her, and through his son's letters felt a sense of her presence. Not that Warren, now eight, was merely a means of remembering his mother. Pershing loved his son, wrote him often, and relished letters from him that sometimes included drawings and schoolwork.

One of Pershing's letters to Warren began,

> I have just had a pretty horseback ride along the Marne. It is a
> beautiful river and has a canal along its entire course . . . This
> morning I rode along the banks for about two miles and came
> to a point where the canal runs across the river and into a tun-
> nel through a mountain . . . The only thing that was lacking
> this morning in making my ride a complete joy was that you
> were not here to go with me.[2]

Seeing children on the street or in a room could make the general choke up suddenly at the thought of his boy so far away, or of his late daughters.

Warren wrote back about sleeping on the porch in the summer; the impressive list of fireworks he got for $1.50; the measles, which prompted his father to assure him, "You won't have to have them again"; riding his bicycle; scoring a hundred on a test; and washing his pony. Senator Warren wrote from Cheyenne that his grandson had become an excellent rider who could keep up with the hired hands. Pershing cherished these letters and put them carefully away. His own went out on his official stationery, typed by a clerk and cleared by military censors like all the rest of the mail.

Other than Warren and Micheline, Pershing's closest attachment was to Charlie Dawes. They had been friends for thirty years. Both were successful men of action. And both had been touched by personal tragedy. Dawes's only child, a son, had drowned on a vacation trip. Sometimes when they were together, something would remind them of their lost children at the same time; their eyes would brim with tears as they exchanged looks without speaking. When Dawes spent the night with Pershing in Paris, the two would take early walks together in their pajamas. To Pershing he was one of the most important men in the war effort, though he never settled into the military lifestyle. "Charlie," Pershing told him, "I once thought I would follow you into law, but I never imagined you would follow me into the army."[3]

Dawes accomplished the impossible every day, scrounging for supplies and transportation, fighting off the bureaucrats in Washington alarmed at the amount of money he was spending. Even so, American troops were becoming frustrated by late pay, poor food, relentless rain and mud, and the complete lack of fighting thus far. Pershing was unhappy with the Allied emphasis on training for defensive warfare and added marksmanship and bayonet drills to the American regimen. He also clarified his position that there would be no grumbling or discouraging talk in the ranks, especially among officers.

Pershing sent a confidential letter on the subject of pessimism to General W. L. Sibert, commander of the First Division, an old friend and a West Point classmate. Their long acquaintance had no effect on his harsh appraisal. He noted that American visitors had heard complaints and pessimistic comments about soldiers' hard living conditions.

> [I]t is not an over statement to say no officer worthy of command would give expression to thoughts of depression . . . a temperament which gives way to weak complaining and querulously protests at hardships such as all soldiers must expect to endure, marks an unfitness for command . . .
>
> The officer who cannot read hope in the conditions that confront us; who is not inspired and uplifted by the knowledge that the heart of our nation is in this war; who shrinks from hardship; who does not exert his personal influence to encourage his men; and who fails in the lofty attitude which should characterize the General who expects to succeed, should yield his position to others with more of our national courage. The consciousness of such an attitude should in honor dictate an application for relief. Whenever the visible effects of it on the command of such an officer reach me in the future, it will constitute grounds for his removal without application.[4]

General Pershing knew the power of optimistic leadership under harsh circumstances. When the American Bible Society asked him to write an introduction for pocket New Testaments being given to his men, he produced a carefully worded balance of stark realism and hope. The introduction also allowed his men a rare glimpse into the general's thoughts about his personal faith and his belief that the world war was a war in defense of Christian ideals.

> To the American soldier:
>
> Aroused against a nation waging war in violation of all Christian principles, our people are fighting in the cause of liberty. Hardship will be your lot, but trust in God will give you comfort; temptation will befall you, but the teachings of our Savior will give you strength. Let your valor as a soldier and your conduct as a man be an inspiration to your comrades and an honor to your country.[5]

By the fall of 1917 there were four divisions of Americans in France, enough men with enough training to see their first action on the front. Pershing decided the First Division, which had been the first to arrive, would go into one- and two-battalion rotations for ten days. Once the Germans learned the untested Americans were in place, they mounted a strong assault. Before dawn on November 4, the Germans began an artillery bombardment and then advanced on the Americans, who were outnumbered four to one. The fight lasted fifteen minutes, producing the first AEF casualties of the war: three killed, five wounded, and a dozen taken prisoner. Pershing wept at the news.

As winter weather set in and battle action tapered off, the general held to his plan of assembling and training troops, building his supply organization, and sparring with French and British authorities over amalgamation. After the fall of the czarist government in the spring of 1917, German troops on the Russian front had withdrawn in July and headed west, pausing to knock out Allied resistance from the Italians fighting in Austria. A formal treaty was signed the following March. After that the entire German war machine could be arrayed against the exhausted and decimated British and French, and against the untried and seemingly timid Americans.

Nine months after declaring war on Germany, with plans to have a million-man army in the field, the United States had only 175,000 troops in Europe, many of them building warehouses or offloading war supplies at the ports. The Allies kept up their desperate argument for Pershing to release American soldiers to French and British units. They renewed their claim that this would save the United States having to buy and ship all the material necessary to support independent American divisions. It would also give the Americans combat experience for a time in the future when American units were up and running, though they never said when this might be. Publicly, Pershing reaffirmed his longstanding position that a sense of national identity, not to mention a presidential directive, demanded a separate American force. Furthermore, an independent America would have more influence in peace negotiations after the war.

A more practical reason was that Pershing remained horrified at the Allied tactics that sacrificed so many men for so little gain. Even British prime minister Lloyd George was dragging his feet in sending new men to fight because his own generals were so wasteful of human life. Not only would the effect of massive American losses under foreign leadership be devastating militarily, the political fallout would send heads rolling all over Washington, beginning with President Wilson's.

No less than General Pétain, whom Pershing admired and considered a friend, complained that Pershing wasn't up to the task. Critics crossed over to Washington to complain relentlessly about the AEF leader's resistance to amalgamation and warn that the war was about to be lost because of it. To settle the issue once and for all, Secretary of War Baker sent General Tasker Bliss, the army chief of staff, to meet with the Allies and hear them out.

When Bliss arrived in London there were more than two hundred thousand Americans in Europe, with thousands more on the way. Many had volunteered while others were drafted under the Selective Service Act passed by Congress a month after war was declared. By the time he met with Pershing and the Supreme War Council in January 1918, General Bliss was leaning toward the view that Americans should man French and British units. He said as much in the meeting, exposing a crack in the formerly solid wall against amalgamation. That night in private, Pershing argued passionately with the army chief to hold steady. Bliss suggested they present both positions to Washington and let them decide. Pershing exclaimed, "We would both be relieved of further duty in France and that is exactly what we should deserve."[6]

In the council the next day, British and French generals retraced their arguments again. Pershing was able to control his anger until the last, when he burst out with a declaration that he would not be pressured into accepting their plan. Thinking Bliss was on their side, the Allied generals asked for his view. "Pershing will speak for both of us and whatever he says with regard to the disposition of American troops will have my approval," Bliss replied.[7] Final as it sounded, the argument was not yet over.

As the weather improved and her armies massed along the Western front, Germany prepared to strike a final blow that would carry them to Paris and victory. For Pershing and the Allies, the wait ended on March 21, 1918, when a massive German force attacked weakened British divisions near the River Somme. The assault began with withering artillery fire and poison gas along more than forty miles of trenches where the front had scarcely moved in three years. For the first time in the West, the Germans used the Hutier advance that had been so effective against Russia and Italy. The Hutier maneuver began with an all-out bombardment, after which advancing columns overran the British lines, avoiding hardened defenses and pockets of resistance to get quickly to the rear, destroying supply lines, artillery emplacements, communications, and transportation capability. Other waves of attackers followed, snuffing out all remaining defensive forces.

The Germans stormed almost forty miles toward the town of Armiens, a key rail depot and major supply center for the entire British front. The British, further weakened by 164,000 new casualties, prepared to fall back to the channel ports where they would make a last stand, while the French planned to break away from Allied positions in a desperate defense of Paris. Government officials began packing for evacuation to Bordeaux.

On April 9 the Germans attacked again, moving against the channel ports to cut off British supply lines and their path of escape. General Douglas Haig called on the French for support and solemnly told his men, "With our backs to the wall, and believing in the justice of our cause, each one of us must fight on to the end." Inspiring though it was, Pershing considered it a sign of desperation. General Pétain predicted the British would surrender within two weeks. Pershing received the news during a visit to now-general Douglas MacArthur, who had been First Captain of his class at West Point as Pershing had been of his. "We old First Captains, Douglas, must never flinch," he said.[8]

Under protest the British continued ferrying American soldiers from Liverpool across the English Channel at the rate of more than one hundred thousand a month. They were incensed to be using their limited shipping capacity, shrunken by U-boat attacks, to transport soldiers who weren't fighting. At a contentious meeting of the War Council in May, French general Ferdinand Foch demanded to know whether Pershing would risk the French being driven all the way to the Loire. "Yes," Pershing said emphatically, "I am willing to take the risk. Moreover, the time may come when the American army will have to stand the brunt of this war, and it is not wise to fritter away our resources in this manner." At the end of the meeting he slammed his fist on the table and declared, "Gentlemen, I have thought this over very deliberately and will not be coerced!"[9]

Resolute as Pershing was about amalgamation, he also knew he had to act soon. A year into their war effort the United States had recorded fewer than two hundred battle deaths. By contrast, twenty thousand British soldiers had died in a single day, July 1, 1916, in the Battle of the Somme. Pershing decided the time had come for the first American offensive of the war. He ordered the First Division to pull men out of a relatively quiet part of the line and take the town of Cantigny, pushing back a two-mile German salient into Allied territory. German artillery-men used a ridge there as an observation post. The French had taken and lost the ridge twice. Americans would take and hold it. Speaking to divisional officers before the battle, Pershing said, "Our people today are hanging expectant upon your deeds. Our future part in this conflict depends upon your actions . . . I hope the standard you set will be high. I know it will be high."[10]

Still arguing for amalgamation, the British prime minister had warned Pershing, "We will refer this to your president."

"Refer and be damned," Pershing replied.[11]

General Robert Lee Bullard assigned his Twenty-eighth Regiment under Colonel Hanson Ely to take the objective, sup-ported by French air cover and artillery. At 4:45 on the morning of May 18, 1918, the first American offensive of the war began with a barrage of heavy guns and mortars. Two hours later Colonel Ely and his men advanced, coming upon two German regiments—one leaving the field as their relief arrived—and rolled forward through the streets. They took the town in forty-five minutes and then continued on to the ridge. By 8:15 the town was secure. As many of them knew, the French had also taken Cantigny back in 1914 only to lose it shortly after. America's reputation, the justification for her delay in fighting, and possibly the fate of amalgamation all depended on holding on to this quaint northern French farm town.

The Germans mounted three counterattacks that day, relent-lessly bombarding the Twenty-eighth. Americans were hampered by the fact that as soon as their offensive ended the French pulled out their artillery to support French troops elsewhere on the front. Americans held their gain until firing stopped for the night. The next day the Germans staged three more attacks, the AEF countering the pounding artillery as best they could with small arms. Major Theodore Roosevelt Jr., son of the former president, commanded a battalion of the Twenty-sixth Infantry called in to shore up the American lines. Along with the German shelling and small-arms counterattacks, the soldiers had to deal with the sight of swollen bodies turning black in the sun, shortages of food and water that were impossible to supply under the circumstances, and the lice that seemed to infest every square foot of ground.

Out of thirty-five hundred men, the Twenty-eighth suffered more than a thousand casualties, almost one soldier in three, including nearly two hundred dead. But they stood their ground. Finally the Germans gave up and retired from the field. Hearing news of his men's steadfastness in action and their success where the French had failed, Pershing pounded his fist on the table and shouted, "I am going to jump down the throat of the next person who asks me, will the Americans really fight!"[12]

ELEVEN

Turning the Tide

THE FRENCH ARTILLERY covering the American attack at Cantigny had withdrawn to redeploy farther south. Their firepower could not save the French army from the onslaught of German lines closing in on the capital. The enemy marched across the Chemin des Dames, a formerly quiet sector in the southwest used as a rest area by both sides. They rolled across the Aisne and the Vesle on their way to the Marne River and Paris. By the end of May 1918, General Pershing realized he would have to send his men into the French ranks to give them any chance of holding out. The Germans gouged a hole in the defensive line thirty miles wide and thirty deep at a cost of another one hundred thousand French casualties. The British, struggling to make their own stand at the channel ports, could offer no reinforcements.

Along the front near the town of Château-Thierry, soldiers of the Third U.S. Infantry Division passed civilians hurrying the other way with whatever they could carry. Scattered among the retreating farmers and shopkeepers were French soldiers in clusters of three or four. Among the French military leaders, only General Pétain seemed convinced his army could be revived. When he appealed to Pershing for Americans to fight alongside his flagging line, Pershing sent them. It was a slight diversion from his absolute rejection of amalgamation, but he agreed to put American soldiers under French command as long as there was no other choice, and as long as AEF divisions fought as a unit.

Pershing threw his Second and Third Divisions into battle against the Germans approaching the Marne. To man the line, Colonel George C. Marshall armed two battalions of cooks, drivers, and other noncombatants and sent them forward with the single directive: "You are to die east of the rail line."[1] Even at this late date, desperate French commanders tried to promote a battle plan calling for the American divisions to split into regiments in the field, producing de facto amalgamation. Probably the French commander on the front, General Degoutte, expected that in such an acute crisis the Americans wouldn't stop to argue.

Degoutte had not counted on the chief of staff of the Second, Colonel Preston Brown. The commander of the Second, General Omar Bundy, opposed the idea of splitting up his men but raised no objection. Colonel Brown spoke up and told the French commander there was no way Americans were going into the line by regiment as each one arrived. They would form a second line behind the French, giving them cover to fall back, and then form a new front. Degoutte asked Brown if he really thought the Americans could hold back the German advance. "General," Brown shot back, "these are American regulars. In a hundred and fifty years they have never been beaten. They will hold."[2]

The German assault on Château-Thierry lasted eighty-two hours. Paris was forty-five miles down the road; the invaders were nearly on its doorstep after four grueling years of fighting. But the Americans held, while the French defenders melted away to the rear, mumbling, *"Tout est perdu!"* ("All is lost!") Writers would call June 1, 1918, the day the Yanks saved Paris. General Foch said as much to Pershing. The American Second Division, including its brigade of Marines commanded by Pershing's former chief of staff, General James Harbord, stopped the major German offensive cold. Germany had hoped to strike a fatal blow in the west before the Americans were ready to oppose them. They had failed.

French orders came up the line for the Marines to fall back and dig trenches in the rear. General Harbord ignored the directive and commanded his men to hold their ground, hollowing out shallow fighting positions with their bayonets. On June 3 the Germans advanced out of Belleau Wood, where they had fallen back under cover after their failed attack on Château-Thierry. The Marines stopped them again, despite continued warnings from retreating Frenchmen that they should follow suit, that *tout est perdu*. A Marine captain in the Second, Lloyd Williams, shouted after them defiantly, "Retreat? Hell, we just got here!"[3]

Pershing had said long before that his men were not trained to fight a defensive action. That was not the American way. True to his word, the AEF went on offense once more with Marines leading the charge. At 3:45 a.m. on June 6, as the Germans were planning yet another counterattack, the Marine brigade and the French 167th Division moved forward. The Marines planned to take the ridge overlooking the battlefield and also occupy Belleau Wood. Crossing a wheat field between their defensive positions and the edge of the forest, the Marines came under attack from dug-in German infantry the American scouts had failed to detect.

Despite heavy casualties, the Allies advanced. By 5:00 p.m. they were in the woods where they traded attacks and counterattacks day after bloody day. U.S. troops were raked with machine-gun fire and bombarded with deadly mustard gas. General Erich Ludendorff hoped to break the Americans' will, hitting them harder than the French and sending his best divisions against them. For all the firepower the Germans turned against the AEF, the army and Marines kept gaining ground foot by foot, sometimes through hand-to-hand combat with bayonets, sometimes with fists. At last, on June 26, the Marines sent a message to Pershing at headquarters: "This Wood now exclusively U.S. Marine Corps."

General Pershing went to visit hospitals where soldiers wounded in the Battle of Belleau Wood were convalescing. The cost of the victory in human terms was high: nearly ten thousand casualties including more than eighteen hundred killed. Some had been blinded by gas; others were missing arms or legs. Pershing praised their bravery and sacrifice, holding his composure throughout his stay. In the car on the way back to headquarters he started to cry, distraught at the pain and sacrifice his orders had required of these men. He told his friend Charlie Dawes that he hoped God would be good to them. There would be more orders and more wounded patriots. Germany was halted in its tracks but still far from beaten.

American soldiers poured into Europe, sometimes as many as ten thousand a day. Pershing had his million men in uniform and more. AEF forces had proven they could stop the Germans when no one else could. The Yanks had driven them out of Cantigny and Château-Thierry; they were ready now to drive them completely out of France. Pershing oversaw his immense, widely scattered command from a private eight-car train complete with power plant, kitchen, bedrooms, offices, and a library. He seemed to relish being completely immersed in leading his army. He kept a close eye on every detail as always. Commanders who seemed hesitant or inept were quickly relieved and sent to a camp at Blois—"went blooey," as the men called it. Charlie Dawes wrote in his diary, "I never saw General Pershing looking or feeling better. He is sleeping well. He is tremendously active."[4]

To the public back home in the United States, Pershing became the face of American honor, righteous indignation, and moxie. Reporters and commentators had softened his old West Point nickname, rechristening him "Black Jack" Pershing. Where the Civil War and other U.S. wars produced constellations of popular leaders and heroes, this war seemed at times personified by a single figure. Some in Washington thought he should consider a run for the presidency. Senator Warren chided him lightheartedly that it was a bad idea, warning that the presidential bug was "worse than moths, caterpillars, and other things that make a bad mess." Pershing answered that he had no interest whatsoever in politics. "As for the presidential bug, it is perfectly ridiculous. I should consider myself very much of an ass if I gave it one moment's consideration."[5]

No amount of work or responsibility kept him from writing to his sisters, May and Bess, and to Warren. The general's fame had made his son a celebrity, a situation Pershing despised and entreated his sisters to keep as low-key as possible. He wanted Warren to be treated like every other boy, and he was irritated to learn a picture had appeared in newspapers across the country of him dressed in a miniature army uniform being saluted by four grade school classmates. "I'm going to be a real soldier when I grow up, just like my dad is," Warren declared in the article. "Dad says that if I were a few years older I could go with him now and help lick the Germans."[6]

The Germans launched another all-out attack on Château-Thierry. Their initial strike failed because the Allies learned about it ahead of time and French artillery smashed the German positions. At midnight on July 15 they hit again, battering the Third Division dug in along the Marne east of Château-Thierry. In addition to achieving his immediate military objective, General Ludendorff believed it was essential for Americans to feel the sting of defeat. They had to be humbled, had to start second-guessing themselves for the Germans to recover. His march toward victory had been halted. This might be his last chance to crush the AEF before the Yanks forced him to retreat.

After three and a half hours of artillery bombardment, the Germans advanced with machine guns and infantry, pinpointing one company of the Thirty-eighth Regiment, Third Division, as the spot where they would pierce the American lines. The company commander, Captain Jesse Wooldridge, concentrated his men and deployed them one platoon after another in the Germans' path. A regiment of Germans quickly overpowered the first platoon on the riverbank. The second platoon slowed them considerably but they finally broke through. The third platoon made its stand, stopping attackers with hand-to-hand fighting. The exhausted Germans who made it past the third platoon were swept up by the fourth, which had been deployed along with the third.

Captain Wooldridge wrote,

It's God's truth that one Company of American solders beat and routed a full regiment of picked shock troops of the German army . . . At ten o'clock . . . the Germans were carrying back wounded and dead from the river bank and we in our exhaustion let them do it—they carried back all but six hundred which we counted later and fifty-two machine guns . . . We had started with 251 men and 5 lieutenants . . . I had left 51 men and 2 second lieutenants.[7]

With the Germans knocked back on their heels at last, Pershing recommended to the French that they launch an attack of their own to cut German supply lines near Soissons, sixty miles from Paris. By July 4, 1918, Pershing had five divisions in the region organized under I Corps command of General Hunter Liggett at Château-Thierry. It was the first time an American corps controlled its own section of the Allied line. On July 18 Pershing and the French unleashed their forces; the American forces included Pershing's old command of Buffalo Soldiers and the French forces included the First Moroccan Division with its famous French foreign legion. The Allies advanced eight miles in two days, sustaining heavy casualties.

Major General Charles Summerall, now commander of the First Division, surely won Pershing's admiration during a discussion with a French officer who wondered if the Division could continue in the face of its heavy losses. "Sir," Summerall answered, "when the First Division has only two men left, they will be echeloned in depth and attacking towards Berlin." To a battalion commander who reported being stopped by the enemy, Summerall replied, "You may have paused for reorganization, but if you ever send me a message with the word stopped in it again you will be relieved of command."[8]

Even as the fighting raged, General Pershing held to his standards of dress and bearing. To him the soldier who was attentive and self-disciplined in his appearance would be equally so facing a German with fixed bayonet. Besides, wherever he was, a soldier in uniform represented the dignity of the United States. Officers were held to the highest standard. The general's aide sent a message to the commander of the Thirty-second Division: "General Pershing directs me to inform you that during the visit he recently made to your division he noted that some of your regimental commanders wore soiled clothing, were unshaven and presented generally an untidy appearance. The commander in chief directs that you give this matter prompt and energetic attention."[9]

Hearing that AEF soldiers had in some cases taken the French advice and deserted the battle line, Pershing's directive to division commanders was immediate and unequivocal: "When men run away in front of the enemy, officers should take summary action to stop it, even to the point of shooting men down who are caught in such disgraceful conduct. No orders need be published on the subject."[10]

By July 22 the First Division had captured the railroad and highway crucial to enemy resupply, and the Germans had retreated. Pershing was beside himself at the news. He exclaimed to General Harbord that "even if neither the First and Second Divisions should ever fire another shot, they had made themselves and their commanders immortal." The Germans would never mount another offensive in the war and knew the tide had suddenly and drastically turned. As German chancellor Georg von Hertling later expressed it, "We expected great events in Paris for the end of July. That was on the 15th. On the 18th even the most optimistic among us understood that all was lost. The history of the world was played out in three days."[11]

The night the battle of Château-Thierry began, Pershing had had dinner with Dorothy Canfield Fisher, an old acquaintance from University of Nebraska days, the chancellor's daughter who had been his student in mathematics and fencing. She was in France and came to see the general whenever their schedules allowed. As Pershing's wife had done, Dorothy endorsed the Montessori teaching method. She had worked with Dr. Maria Montessori in Rome. She was also earning a reputation as an educator and author in her own right. During the dinner conversation she asked the general if he really thought the Americans could stop the seemingly invincible German advance.

"You're not asking me that question seriously, are you?" he responded playfully. "You don't mean me to understand that you are employing the English language to express *doubt* in the matter? Why, child, *of course* we're going to beat them!" On their earlier visits the general had seemed somber and worried about their prospects. Now he acted confident and happy. "The old charm, the old light-hearted sunniness were there again," she observed.[12]

The Allied action beginning at Cantigny and ending at Soissons had cost the Germans all the ground they'd gained during the spring. Pershing now had to decide the best way to capitalize on their success. On August 10, 1918, the general formally created the American First Army. By then there were as many American soldiers in Europe—1.2 million—as there were British and nearly as many as there were French. After consultation with Foch and Pétain, the Allies decided that the First Army would attack the German salient at St. Mihiel. This was a triangular bulge with its base along twenty-five miles of front line. From there the Germans had pressed sixteen miles into French territory, capturing the town of St. Mihiel at the tip of the triangle. Germans had occupied the salient since 1914 and were deeply dug in, despite numerous French efforts to uproot them.

On August 30 General Foch called on General Pershing at First Army field headquarters in Ligny-en-Barrois. Since August 6 Foch had held the title of Marshal of France. The French commander—short, round-faced, balding, and with an infectious grin under his big mustache when circumstances allowed—explained his master plan of attack for the region, which included splitting the American army into two groups with French soldiers in between and putting it under operational control of the French Fourth Army.

Amalgamation again! The French army had been throwing down its arms and deserting. Before that it had barely survived a mutiny. Now it seemed Foch wanted the Americans to do the fighting and the French to get the credit. With the size of the American force now in place and its proven success on the battlefield, the suggestion was not only ludicrous but insulting.

Pershing held his temper at first. He told Foch that his proposal "virtually destroys the American Army that we have been trying so long to form." Foch said he regretted the situation, but that was the way it had to be. Pershing offered to relieve a large section of the front so the Americans could fight as a unit under his command.

Foch waved off the suggestion and, dripping sarcasm, asked, "Do you wish to take part in the battle?" Pershing and the Americans had saved France from ruin. Foch himself had said so. Now this.

Struggling for control, Pershing answered, "Most assuredly, but as an American Army and in no other way!"

"There is no time to send an entire Army."

"Give me a sector [of the front] and I will occupy it immediately . . . wherever you say."

Foch went on to criticize the American shortage of artillery. Furious, Pershing reminded him that the French and British governments had begged the United States to spend shipping capacity on men and machine guns rather than artillery, and that Foch had promised he would make up the shortfall from Allied reserves. Foch came back again to the sense of urgency. There was no time to get the American Army in place; therefore, they must serve under the French.

When Pershing failed to budge, Foch huffed, "Your French and English comrades are going into battle; are you coming with them?"

All control now lost, Pershing raged at the Frenchman, "Marshal Foch, you have no authority as Allied commander-in-chief to call upon me to yield up my command of the American Army and have it scattered among the Allied forces where it will not be an American Army at all!"

"I must insist upon that arrangement," Foch demanded.

"Marshal Foch you may insist all you please, but I decline absolutely to agree to your plan. While our army will fight wherever you may decide, it will not fight except as an independent American army!"

In his diary that night, Pershing wrote, "Firmly convinced that it is the fixed purpose of the French, and perhaps the British, that the formation of an American Army should be prevented if possible. Perhaps they do not want America to find out her strength."[13]

As he left the meeting with Pershing, Foch, pale and shaken, told the American, "Once you have thought more about it I am sure you will consent." Evidently the French commander still understood neither the man nor his commitment to doing what he believed was right. The next day, with Pétain supporting his view, Pershing proposed to Foch that the Americans expand their sector to include the whole line between the Meuse River and the Argonne Forest. They would take positions there after pushing the Germans out of the St. Mihiel salient, sixty miles away. Foch agreed but wanted to have the Americans in position to start the Meuse-Argonne advance on September 25, ahead of the colder weather. The challenge for Pershing and his First Army was to dislodge the Germans from positions they had held for four years, move half a million troops sixty miles, and then be ready for the biggest offensive of the war in a matter of days—or hours—after reaching the Meuse-Argonne line.

Pershing agreed. As he explained later, "It was only my absolute faith in the energy and resourcefulness of our officers of both staff and line and the resolute and aggressive courage of our soldiers that permitted me to accept such a prodigious undertaking."[14] He and his staff immediately began planning two major offensives less than three weeks apart, the first less than two weeks away. No one at that point dared hope that in little more than ten weeks, it would all be over.

TWELVE

Victoire!

TO DEFEAT THE invaders who had held St. Mihiel since the first months of the war, General Pershing amassed an army of 550,000 American soldiers. He also had 110,000 French troops, more than 3,000 heavy guns, an air force of 1,400 airplanes, and a tank brigade under his former aide and one-time prospective brother-in-law, Colonel George Patton. The Allied advance began with a deafening artillery assault at an hour past midnight, September 12, 1918. At five o'clock the infantry charged into the heavily fortified positions, negotiating barbed wire, booby traps, and a sheet of machine-gun fire.

It was the first American offensive in history to combine artillery, infantry, air support, and tank warfare. Pershing had planned everything down to the last detail and issued meticulous orders that coordinated the massive movement for maximum synergy. It was a masterpiece of order and precision—the troops in their proper places, effectively led, and as well supplied as could be expected under the circumstances. Pershing seemed always to be in the front lines, and his officer corps followed his example. The sight of their leaders sharing the risks was a powerful inspiration to enlisted ranks preparing to run toward the muzzles of German machine guns. A French study of why Americans could negotiate German barbed wire so easily concluded it was because of their long legs and big feet. It failed to mention the special training of engineers for the task and bridges of chicken wire placed over the barbs.

By the end of the day, Pershing's force had taken two hundred square miles of territory and sixteen thousand prisoners. The general's insistence on waiting until he was ready and then fighting with American units intact was completely vindicated. The St. Mihiel offensive was a military triumph. The next day, his fifty-eighth birthday, General Pershing walked with General Pétain through the streets of St. Mihiel. "We gave them a d--- good licking, didn't we?"[1] Pershing asked. Town residents, some streaming tears, rushed out to thank their liberators after four years of occupation.

Even before all the fighting ended in the St. Mihiel salient, Pershing and his master planner, Colonel George C. Marshall, were executing the almost impossible task of repositioning the American army and its supporting forces for the Meuse-Argonne campaign. There the Allied strength would be almost twice what it had been in St. Mihiel, more than a million soldiers. Their objective was to push the German army away from the rail lines at Sedan that carried 250 trains a day full of supplies.

There were only three roads between St. Mihiel and the Meuse-Argonne region. A single division could occupy twenty miles of road, and Pershing had to march in fifteen divisions while somehow making room for the eleven French divisions they were replacing to march out. While cleaning up on one front and moving to another, the Americans also built airfields, rail lines, forty-four hospitals, and eighty supply depots. Units got lost, draft animals died of exhaustion in their traces, and trucks broke down and got stuck in the mud. Pershing sent a hoard of young staff officers into the field to find bottlenecks and clear them at all cost. Their superhuman effort was a factor in every American division being in place on time.

Pershing had surrounded himself with officers like himself: fearless, decisive, plain-spoken, inspiring, intelligent. Unfortunately for the American army, there were not nearly enough of these leaders to go around. Nor were there experienced enlisted ranks to replace all the casualties of the last two weeks. Tens of thousands of officers and men were raw recruits; some had only been in the army six weeks, including travel time from Dallas, Hoboken, or wherever they'd signed up. They made mistakes and would, Pershing knew, make many more. Yet the general also believed this was the Allies' moment to wipe out "the Hun," as the dreaded enemy was known. And what the green troops did have was enthusiasm and confidence. That would carry them a long way in the hard weeks ahead.

In the future the general would have to do without his full

complement of airplanes, tanks, and seasoned artillerymen. The French laid claim to half the air support for their own offensive actions elsewhere. There were fewer than two hundred tanks available, about two-thirds of Colonel Patton's command at St. Mihiel. Though he had more than four thousand artillery pieces, the majority were manned by Frenchmen new to their divisions and lightly trained.

Even a million troops and more would have their hands full achieving the First Army's military objective. The AEF was part of an all-out Allied offensive against the Hindenburg Line, a three-hundred-mile-long defensive barrier that cut through the northeast quadrant of France. Built during the winter of 1916–17 by German workers and Russian prisoners of war, the line was a masterpiece of military engineering and a daunting sight to attackers. The first element was a ditch big enough to engulf a tank. Next came a forest of camouflaged barbed wire, then steel-reinforced concrete bunkers and machine-gun emplacements. Behind the bunkers was a network of trenches, then last of all, two lines of artillery. General Harbord considered it "the most comprehensive system of leisurely prepared field defense known to history."[2]

The Allied plan was to attack the Hindenburg Line along three fronts. The northern section would be hit by an army of French, British, and Belgian soldiers marching through Flanders. The central section would be engaged by more British divisions and the armies of the British Empire including Canada, Australia, and New Zealand. The Americans and the rest of the French divisions would come up from the south. The Americans would march along the western bank of the Meuse and then through the Argonne Forest, which Pershing's chief of staff called "the most ideal defensive terrain" he had ever seen.[3] Ground beneath the trees was covered with thick underbrush, ideal for hiding snipers, machine-gun emplacements, and booby traps. The uneven surface, obscured by the undergrowth, was torturous on infantrymen weighed down with rifles, ammunition, gas masks, canteens, emergency rations, and rain slickers. To make matters still worse, hills along the way bristled with German machine guns and artillery.

The American First Army launched its grand offensive in heavy fog at 5:30 on the morning of September 26. Moving out on a twenty-four mile front after a three-hour artillery barrage, they overtook the first of three German forward positions and then punched through four miles to the second German line in some places. The center of Pershing's three corps faltered, its inexperienced troops stopped by reinforced German divisions. Pershing seemed everywhere at once on his private train, encouraging, criticizing, demanding answers and results. On September 28 he visited all three corps commanders doing "all in my power to instill an aggressive spirit into the corps headquarters."[4]

The Germans slowed and then stopped the Allied advance even as casualties mounted. French generals and politicians used the situation as justification for recommending Pershing be removed from command. Clemenceau's chief of staff observed, "All that great body of men which the American Army represented was literally struck with paralysis because the brain didn't exist, because the generals and their staffs lacked experience."[5]

Clemenceau himself visited Pershing the next day and evidently formed the same opinion. Truly Pershing was dealing with massive challenges. Poor roads that made massive troop movements a nightmare in the best of weather had been turned into a quagmire by autumn rains. When their supply trucks and ammunition wagons became hopelessly bogged down, men carried artillery shells forward in their arms through knee-deep mud. Sharing the road with soldiers were ambulances heading for the rear and wagons of every sort bringing up twenty-five thousand tons of supplies a day to the front. Even the worldwide influenza epidemic that year bedeviled Pershing's war effort. By the end of the offensive, more soldiers would die from the flu than from German bullets.

Pershing's exceptional organizational and leadership skills made him uniquely fit to head his Allied army at this moment in history. Under the circumstances no one could have exceeded the performance of Pershing and his crack cadre of officers, including Marshall, MacArthur, and Patton. What the French prime minister Clemenceau saw, however, was justification that he and Foch had been right all along in insisting the Americans fight under French control. He instructed Foch to relieve Pershing of command and replace him with a French general. President Wilson and Secretary Baker had been lobbied relentlessly on the same question.

To their credit, both Americans saw the value of Pershing's leadership and steadfastly refused to take up the argument. On a trip to London, Secretary Baker was called to Lloyd George's sickbed at his country home. The prime minister informed the secretary that General Pershing must be relieved. Baker replied, "Mr. Prime Minister, we are not in need of advice from any foreign nation as to who should lead our armies."[6]

Foch first tried—again—to order French divisions into the middle of the American line. Pershing—again—refused the order and Foch backed down. Days later, Foch sent Pershing orders relieving him of his army command and replacing him with a French general. The next day Pershing went to Foch, furious at so outrageous an insult. Foch backed down again. Heated though their words were, the meeting gave Pershing a chance to present a revised plan of attack, including the formation of an American Second Army. Foch approved Pershing's proposal and that, for the time being, was the end of the discussions on amalgamation.

Meanwhile General Pershing had halted the army's faltering advance to redeploy his most experienced divisions, hoping to improve their progress. During the lull he wrote heartfelt letters to one who seemed always to be on his mind. Even when the fighting was at its worst, he stole a few moments to pen a letter to Micheline in Paris. "I send you a million kisses and I embrace you tenderly," he wrote on September 29. He saw her whenever possible during his official trips to the capital and apologized when he left without a visit: "Do you wish to pardon me—do you wish to give me a long kiss like always and permit me to send you a million thought[s] of chagrin?"[7]

As the Americans paused, the Germans reinforced their troops. When the First Army moved out again on October 4, they met stiff resistance. Machine-gun fire was relentless. Compounding the difficulty was the condition of the roads, by now nothing but rivers of mud and trash. Engineers laid down trails of rocks to support the convoy's weight, with mixed success. As a chilly rain poured down, fifteen thousand American troops caught the flu in one week. Pershing needed eighty thousand soldiers and one hundred thousand horses immediately to make up for his losses.

The general's earlier exuberance had yielded to concentration and concern. He was masterminding an impossibly big, impossibly complex event. He lived aboard his train, visiting corps and division headquarters, keeping close watch over the battle, scrutinizing maps, reading reports, and issuing orders until past midnight. He seemed tired. He was graying rapidly, clearly burdened with decisions and responsibilities no one else could shoulder. No matter how he felt, with the exception of a handful of close friends like Charlie Dawes, he never let feelings of worry or exhaustion show. As he admonished Colonel Marshall, "A commander, no matter how weary, should never be seen burying his head on his desk, lest someone interpret it as a loss of hope. He must always give the impression of optimism."[8]

The battle seemed deadlocked as the First Army kept fighting against a solidly entrenched foe. Both sides needed massive numbers of replacement troops. American soldiers were now crossing the Atlantic at the rate of three hundred thousand per month. By contrast, the Germans were running short of manpower. Determined to break the deadlock and move forward to victory, Pershing rearranged his command, elevating two of his most trusted and accomplished generals to high positions. He formed the Second Army under Lieutenant General Robert Lee Bullard. General Bullard, who was fluent in French, had served with Pershing in the Philippines. Earlier in the war he had said privately that he thought Pershing was too much of a pacifist to lead an army because he had gone to such lengths to avoid fighting the Moros. By this time he had long since changed his mind.

Pershing also appointed Lieutenant General Hunter Liggett to take Pershing's place as commander of the First Army. Like Pershing and Bullard, Liggett had served in the American West, the Spanish-American War, and the Philippines, where Captain George C. Marshall had been his aide de camp. With Bullard leading the First Army and Liggett heading the Second, Pershing could leave the details to these distinguished officers and focus his attention on theater-wide strategy and the supply and infrastructure he knew were essential to victory.

The armies renewed their advance until October 19, when Pershing ordered another pause to consolidate his forces. The First Army had lost another one hundred thousand soldiers, and another one hundred thousand were separated from the main columns—lost, injured, or missing in action. Still they marched forward, exiting the Argonne Forest at the end of October. Remembering those days after the war, Colonel Marshall wrote to Pershing:

> With distressingly heavy casualties, disorganized and only partially trained troops, supply problems of every character due to the devastated zone so rapidly crossed, inclement and cold weather, flu, stubborn resistance by the enemy on one of the strongest positions of the Western Front, pessimism on all sides and pleadings to halt the battle made by many

of the influential members of the army, you persisted in your
determination to force the fighting over all the difficulties and
objections . . . nothing else in your leadership throughout was
comparable to this.[9]

As hard as the Americans had it, the Germans were in worse shape
and they knew it. Replacement soldiers were now schoolboys and
the wounded ordered out of their hospital beds. On October 30
Germany's ally Austria-Hungary surrendered. Turkey laid down
their arms four days later.

As the Allies began discussing peace terms among themselves, British field marshal Douglas Haig proposed generous
terms that the Germans would readily accept. Foch and Pétain
held out for a less accommodating stance but still a negotiated peace. Pershing, who had not been invited to the meeting,
declared afterward that anything less than unconditional surrender was a tragic mistake, leaving Germany free to rearm and
make another attempt to dominate her neighbors. In a private
meeting later he exclaimed, "We have the upper hand, and there
is no reason why the terms shouldn't be stiff enough to prevent a war such as this from ever having to be fought again."[10]
His plainspokenness represented a soldier's perspective on the
military solution, without considering the political climate in
Washington. An emissary sent by President Wilson to meet with
the Supreme War Council pressed Pershing to step away from
his position. Privately he still seethed at the thought of so much
blood buying anything less than complete surrender and the
prospect of Germany recovering from her losses to strike again.

With peace negotiations under way, General Pershing turned his attention to winning the war. In a matter of days he reshaped and revived his legions. The army was retrained in coordinating with artillery and using poison gas, leaders were reassigned, and the units prepared for a final assault. Leading divisions were manned by seasoned battle veterans headed by the army's most capable officers. As peace negotiations and the war offensive reached fever pitch, Pershing was also fighting the flu and a raging toothache. The dentist's only solution was morphine, which Pershing refused because, he said, "I have too much need of all my senses." He added, "The best I can do is swear. It seems to relieve me a little bit."[11]

The Americans began another push on November 1. Infantry, artillery, and air cover coordinated seamlessly and the Germans were in full retreat. The First Army advanced so rapidly it ran off the general's maps. On November 5 Foch tried once more, in vain, to assign American divisions to the French army. In a gesture to the French army's national pride, when the German rail depot at Sedan fell at last to the Allies on November 6, the American First Division held back and allowed the French Fourth Army to enter the city alone.

In the end there was an armistice, not a surrender of the sort General Pershing advocated. The night of November 10, Allies received word that the armistice would be signed at five o'clock the next morning aboard a railroad car in the Compiègne Forest and go into effect at eleven. Pershing's staff stayed up all night celebrating—with their champagne on ice in a German helmet—then drove to Pershing's office at Chaumont at six in the morning on November 11. They found their commander-in-chief alone at his desk. At 11:00 a.m. the guns went silent and the war was over. *Victoire!*

No doubt everyone in the room that morning agreed with German field marshal Paul von Hindenburg, who later wrote, "The American infantry in the Argonne won the war."[12]

THIRTEEN

General of the Armies

THE END OF the "war to end all war" did not mark the end of
General Pershing's responsibilities in Europe. The vast American
army had to be demobilized and transported back across the
Atlantic. Until then they still had to be fed, paid, sheltered, doc-
tored, and kept sufficiently busy to stay out of trouble. Battalions
drilled and drilled some more, the general always on the lookout for missing buttons or a rusty bayonet. The AEF organized
theatrical performances, athletic competitions, horse shows, and
classroom instruction, including college level courses. Pershing
gave scores of speeches to troops waiting to sail home, thanking
them for their service.

General Pershing loved his men for their bravery and sacrifice
and considered it his duty to take care of them. He attended many

award ceremonies to present battle decorations. As he pinned on a medal or tied a battle ribbon to a regimental flag, his eye took in every detail. After a review of the Forty-second Division, he wrote its officers, "The men were not so well set up physically, and their clothing showed lack of proper care."[1] At the end of the war as at the beginning, the vast majority of soldiers saw Black Jack Pershing as a starchy, humorless fault-finder. His friends still knew the warm and tenderhearted man who could cry over wounded infantrymen. His peers and superiors in Europe and Washington knew him as a leader of historic ability and dedication. The American public looked at Black Jack Pershing and saw a hero.

Shortly before Christmas 1918, the general took his first leave since sailing from New York. He spent a week in Monte Carlo for golf, Turkish baths, and walks along the beach. Then it was back to maintaining discipline and order among the two million Americans in uniform who were in Europe when the armistice was signed. He had promised his son he could come visit him in France when the war was over. Young Warren sailed over with Secretary Baker, the new American ambassador to France, and a group of congressmen coming for an inspection tour. They traveled aboard the S.S. *Leviathan*, formerly the *Imperator*, flagship of the German Atlantic liner fleet. At 950 feet and 54,000 tons, the three-funnel steamship was the largest passenger vessel in the world when it was launched in 1913. She was in New York Harbor when war broke out between Germany and England. The American government commandeered it as a troop ship, and was now using it to ferry as many as fourteen thousand men home per voyage, ten times its capacity as a luxury liner.

Young Warren and the congressional delegation arrived at the French port of Brest on March 14, 1919. That morning, General Pershing reviewed six thousand soldiers waiting to sail for home. In the afternoon he took a tender out to the ship for a joyful reunion with the son he had not seen in two years. Pershing and the boy were inseparable from then until they returned to America together six months later.

Often Warren wore a specially made lieutenant's uniform. After a while he decided he'd rather be a sergeant, so the officer shoulder boards were removed from his jacket and sergeant stripes sewn on. He stood on reviewing stands beside his father and walked with him along ranks of soldiers, returning their salute just as his father did. Once at a party the general received a telephone call. An officer looking for him found him in a room off to the side, watching Warren sleep. "I like to be with my boy," he said. "I have seen so little of him in the last few years that it seems as if we hardly know each other. I want to see all of him I can. I wouldn't feel right if I let the evening pass without spending part of it with my son, even if he is asleep."[2]

He had worried that his sisters would be too protective, that they would spoil Warren, and that his own notoriety would make Warren prideful or conceited. He needn't have. Warren was a good-natured, well-adjusted boy; polite, adventurous, at ease under any circumstances. The general took his son on visits to the Duchy of Luxembourg and to meet the Queen of the Belgians. He also introduced Warren to Micheline. They liked each other at once, their friendship cemented by museum visits and trips to the candy store.

Pershing continued his relationship with his mistress as before, begging her to forgive him for being "busy and impatient." He had evidently hurt her feelings in his rush to finish a world war, and he wrote to apologize: "You know me well enough to know that I did not mean anything. It would be a poor kind of love that would not overlook that." He was surprised, he said, that she would cry on the phone when he called, "but I do understand, and shall never again be harsh even in manner—my *heart* isn't harsh anyway."[3]

Part of his busyness stemmed from following through on a list of suggestions and projects he had initiated for his soldiers' benefit. He tracked progress of the Military Police, a force he had seen the need for and brought into being. With so many Americans on the ground there was bound to be occasional trouble with the law. Local police couldn't always handle incidents effectively, soldiers were unfamiliar with statutes and customs on foreign soil, and there was the matter of who had jurisdiction. Pershing believed the army should have its own police force and the Military Police, still a fixture in the military today, was born.

Seeing the terrible toll trench foot took on his soldiers, Pershing supervised development of a redesigned boot. Trench foot was a condition caused when feet stayed wet for hours inside shoes. It produced fungus or blisters and could lead to gangrene and amputation. The simple remedy was to keep feet dry. The army adapted Pershing's new boot design, which featured an extra layer of sole material, more stitching, additional reinforcing rivets, and a more effective and longer-lasting waterproofing compound. Troops wore the Pershing boot until the end of the war, after which the army replaced it with a lighter model when trench warfare ended and such a sturdy, heavy boot was no longer necessary.

A lifelong music lover, Pershing wanted to form an elite marching band that would look and perform to the highest standards. The army formed the new band and also a large precision drill team of more than three thousand. Both groups were called "Pershing's Own."

On Memorial Day, May 30, 1919, General Pershing and Warren attended the dedication of the cemetery of Romagne in the Meuse-Argonne region, where thirty thousand Allied soldiers killed in the Meuse-Argonne campaign were buried. Pershing ended his remarks that day by thanking the fallen: "And now, dear comrades, Farewell. Here, under the clear skies, we leave you forever in God's keeping."[4] The next month, on June 24, Warren celebrated his tenth birthday. For Bastille Day, the French national holiday on July 14, Pershing was one of the guests of honor in a spectacular victory parade in Paris, through the Arc de Triomphe and along the famous Champs-Élysées. The AEF was represented by forty-five regiments still waiting to ship home.

Five days later the general and his son were in London for another round of celebrations. Secretary of State for War Winston Churchill and an honor guard from the Scots Guards waited at the train station to escort them to Buckingham Palace. From there the general took his place in another massive parade, with tens of thousands marching and millions lining the streets of London. They passed in review before King George and Queen Mary. Warren stood with the royal couple in their box; the queen made sure to have her picture taken with him. He told a reporter for the Associated Press that the "big Scotch drum major with the dress on and the high thing on his head"[5] was what he liked most.

The next few days were a whirlwind of British pomp and majesty for the general: lunch with the Lord Mayor of London and his wife; dinner in the House of Commons hosted by Secretary Churchill; lunch with the king and queen in the state dining room at the palace; presentation of a monogrammed dress sword set with diamonds and rubies; honorary degrees from Oxford and Cambridge. Back in Europe, Pershing had lunch with the king of Italy, saw an opera in Verona, and visited Milan and Venice.

Sometime during all the panoply, Nita Patton arrived on advice from her brother George. He thought the general still had feelings for her. "How long are you staying? And what are you going to do over here?" Pershing asked bluntly.[6] She went back home to California, where she asked her family never to mention Pershing again.

The general's heart belonged absolutely to another. From London he wrote Micheline Resco to say that since he had arrived "there isn't a minute that I do not think of you."[7] He said he dreamed of her every night. Even so, and in spite of their two-year affair, he decided against taking her back home to America. He told her she should stay in Paris and pursue her career as an artist.

"My work is finished," he wrote her.

One is not able to stay in a strange country always. You know how I love France and the French, especially my dear one.

You also know how I regret that I am no longer young, but if I were still young I would not have been able to participate in the great war at the head of our army. I am at the end of my life. You are a great artist. You have all your life in the future with a commencement already brilliant.[8]

He told her they would still see each other, and that perhaps she could come to America some day. Micheline likely assumed she would go home with her general. The news that she would not was devastating. Though her reaction didn't change Pershing's mind, it rattled him. He did what he could to soften the shock, writing tenderly that it wasn't the end of the world and that he still loved her and wanted to be with her: "I am not able to stay happy when you are sad. I send you all my kisses and all my love. Always to you."[9]

At last the time came for the general to sail for home. From a skeleton force of two hundred in the spring of 1917 his command had swollen to two million. By the summer of 1919, only a dozen or so remained. A special train took them to the port at Brest, where Marshal Foch and Marshal Pétain waited to see them off on the *Leviathan*. Foch was moved by the sight of Pershing struggling to control his emotions. Bentley Mott, the American military attaché, told Foch that Pershing had never been a cold man but always held himself in reserve as his duty required.

On board, the general occupied the magnificent suite designed for Kaiser Wilhelm. It was there that Warren ran in a few days later when they were at sea to say news had just come over the radio that his father had been promoted to General of the

Armies of the United States, a rank unprecedented in American history. He was authorized six stars, though he never wore them then or later. He did eventually adopt an insignia of four gold stars, as distinct from the four silver stars of a full general.

Pershing stepped ashore at Hoboken, across the Hudson River from Manhattan, on the morning of September 8, 1919. There to welcome him were ranks of honor guards, guns blasting from the harbor, bands, whistles, sirens, foghorns, and bands. Secretary Baker met him at the foot of the gangplank with his commission as General of the Armies. The general handed it to his son, who put it carefully it in his coat pocket. Pershing and his welcoming party rode in an open car though New York as an avalanche of ticker tape and confetti rained down. Schoolchildren had the day off to join in the celebration.

The next day they went to Philadelphia, where the whole city took an official holiday. There he greeted Clara Warren, Senator Warren's vivacious and charming second wife, who traveled with them to Washington. Secretary Baker and Vice President Thomas Marshall met them at Union Station, the beginning of a visit to the capital that would include another spectacular parade and the general addressing a joint session of Congress.

Warren returned to Nebraska to start school. Pershing and his small personal staff turned to the mountain of invitations for the general to endorse, address, or join hundreds of organizations, from the Junior Polo Club of Narragansett Pier and the American Friends of Lafayette to the Anti-Swearing League and the Missouri Negro Soldiers Memorial Society. There were also countless social invitations and personal letters to answer. The granddaughter of Ulysses S. Grant, the first American general to have a level of authority (General of the Army) comparable to Pershing's, wrote that she was "very glad to think my grandfather has had such a great successor."[10]

He received a horse from the American Legion and a Cadillac from General Motors. Eager to relax, he sneaked out of his Washington hotel in civilian clothes for a vacation on Naushon Island near Martha's Vineyard as the guest of a friend. From there he went to the twenty-six-thousand-acre Adirondack estate of a family related to his aide Fox Conner. The closest rail depot was a flag stop seven miles from the house. "They can't get me here,"[11] Pershing observed of the relentless reporters.

The general and his hosts danced, hunted deer, had dinner parties, and drank excellent whiskey despite its being outlawed by Prohibition. After three weeks, his duties called him back to Washington. Congress had asked for a report, the Belgian royal family was coming for a visit, and President Wilson was incapacitated by illness, shifting the burden of entertaining the royals to the general. "Is your little boy too big to kiss?" asked the Belgian queen. "If not, please send him a kiss for me."[12]

Pershing toured cities and military installations across the country, often traveling by private railroad car attached to a scheduled train. Honored as he was, he confided to an aide that he was tired of municipal receptions, aldermen's wives, chicken dinners, and Thousand Island dressing, the last "often three times in a single day."[13] His every move was fodder for reporters. President Wilson was in poor health and Theodore Roosevelt had died in January 1919 ending hope of a political comeback.

Political odds makers looked for signs Pershing would enter the 1920 presidential race.

Exploratory committees gauged public interest; the general said he wasn't seeking the nomination but that "no patriotic American could decline to serve in that high position, if called to do so by the people."[14] Pershing's strongest supporters were politically inexperienced and did not attract the party leaders. It was also true that the American people were tired of war and anything that reminded them of it. The public loved him as a hero but never warmed to him as a politician. Pershing, who had never cared for politics in the first place, was happy to let the matter drop.

As General of the Armies, Pershing had no more battles to fight. Instead, he oversaw a dramatic reduction in American military strength. The war was over, a large army was unnecessary, and it was time to economize. The National Defense Act of 1920 established the idea of an army composed of the regular standing army, the army reserve, and the National Guard. The general encouraged Congress to maintain a regular army of 250,000 troops, plus an even larger number of reserves in National Guard battalions and ROTC units. Later, over Pershing's strong objection, the standing army was reduced to 100,000.

Two relationships loomed large in the general's life after the war, as they had during it. One was Warren. Any letter from him was always on the top of the stack. During school vacations the general took his son with him on inspection trips to the Canal Zone, the Virgin Islands, Puerto Rico, and elsewhere. When they were together they scarcely left each other's side, riding horseback in the mornings, touring during the day, the general drilling Warren in his lessons, teaching him to box, fretting about his health and hereditary bow-leggedness, and tucking him in every night.

The other great presence was Micheline Resco. She and the general kept up their correspondence, their love for each other undimmed by separation. He sent her monthly checks and brought her regularly to Washington, where she stayed in an apartment or hotel near him. The general public knew nothing about Pershing's devoted mistress. Wild rumors circulated that the general was engaged first to one socialite and then another. The *Chicago Tribune* reported that in the month after he returned from France, Pershing was reported to have wedding plans with twenty-three different women.

On July 1, 1921, General of the Armies John J. Pershing was appointed army chief of staff. While he served dutifully in the post until the day he retired, he would be frustrated to realize he was presiding over a disarmament he thought went too far. The army that rescued France from the invincible German fighting machine folded under the onslaught of congressional budget cuts. America wanted to forget about war and lose itself in the Roaring Twenties. Though the general's fighting days were over, he preached vigilance and readiness even in prosperous times. It was advice two American presidents later wished they had heeded.

General Pershing at Arlington Cemetery. He wept at the news of the first American casualties in France and cared deeply for his men. His wish to be buried among them at Arlington was granted when he died in 1948.

Even after his retirement, Pershing was encouraged to continue using his opulent office in the old navy department building.

General Pershing at his desk. For years he was considered by the local media to be Washington's best-dressed man.

Warren Pershing and his wife, the former Muriel Bache Richards, at Washington National Cathedral, Thanksgiving Day, 1938. Her grandfather, Julius Bache, was one of America's most successful financiers; Warren became a millionaire investor in his own right.

General Pershing calls on President Roosevelt at the White House, December 1937. Three months later Pershing was near death from a host of ailments, though he recovered enough to attend Warren's wedding in April 1938 and make a final trip to France the following year.

FOURTEEN

To Truth-telling and to Courage

THE MANDATORY MILITARY retirement age was sixty-four. As General Pershing neared that milestone he showed no signs of slowing down. In 1923 Congress appointed him head of the American Battle Monuments Commission, charged with designing, building, and maintaining monuments on foreign soil to commemorate American sacrifices. This responsibility took him to France regularly, where he toured likely locations for memorials, met with local officials, and considered the various proposed designs. He also spent as much time as possible with Micheline.

Gossip continued to surface that Pershing was going to marry.

He was reportedly seen having dinner with Louise Cromwell Brooks, the same Louise Brooks some accounts had him squiring around years earlier. To complicate matters further, Brooks supposedly had an affair with one of Pershing's aides, promised to marry him, then announced her engagement to Douglas MacArthur. Though MacArthur was already scheduled to sail for the Philippines, the story persisted that Pershing transferred MacArthur because Pershing was still romantically interested in Miss Brooks. MacArthur biographer William Manchester is one who takes this position.

Louise fueled the gossip by telling a reporter, "Jack wanted me to marry him. When I wouldn't, he wanted me to marry one of his colonels. I wouldn't do that. So here I am packing my trunks."

Pershing huffed, "It's all . . . poppycock without the slightest foundation and based on the idlest gossip . . . If I were married to all the ladies to whom the gossips have engaged me I would be a regular Brigham Young."[1]

To maintain military morale in a time of severe budget cuts, the general continued his inspection tours of bases at home and abroad, encouraging capable officers to stay in uniform. He was keenly interested in improving the army education system. In Cuba and the Philippines, Pershing had seen what happened when army officer ranks were filled with men who had no experience leading in battle and no training for it. He believed the army school system, the Command and General School and the Army War College, should concentrate on preparing officers to lead large forces into modern combat. Up until then, the curriculum focused on what was happening in the present. Pershing wanted to train students to fight the wars of the future. This was especially important as senior officers from the Great War left the service and turned the reins over to men without combat experience. Biographer Jim Lacey considered the change in army school teaching "probably his most enduring legacy to the army."[2]

Along with changes in military education, Pershing set up the nation's first permanent general staff, whose only responsibility was to plan for future operations and coordinate those operations when the time came. Both the educational reforms and the general staff were crucial to American mobilization twenty years later at the beginning of World War II.

Pershing's analytical abilities and organizational genius did not prevent him from overlooking important changes in modern warfare. He had seen the military value of airplanes during the Meuse-Argonne offensive and had witnessed a demonstration by American air ace Billy Mitchell showing that bombers could sink a battleship. Even so, he downplayed the potential benefit of a large American air fleet and as chief of staff steered appropriations away from developing it. He took a similar view of tanks. Pershing knew they could be useful in supporting infantry, but the handful of machines he had seen in France were slow and unreliable. He seemed not to recognize the power tanks could have in the field as an independent force. It was somewhat ironic, then, that the army named its first heavy tank the Pershing. Beset by delays, the Pershing would be introduced in the last months of World War II, with military leaders divided over its strategic use and relative value in the face of its forty-six-ton weight and operational limitations.

By 1924, Warren had enrolled at Phillips Exeter Academy, an exclusive boarding school in New Hampshire. The general wasn't satisfied with his progress there and sent him to the Institut Carnall in Switzerland. The fifteen-year-old sailed to Europe that summer, once more aboard the *Leviathan*, now restored to its former luxury and operated by United States Lines. He stopped in Paris, where Micheline took him to see the sights, and then went on to his school in the town of Rolle.

On September 13 of that year, General of the Armies Pershing retired. He remained chairman of the Monuments Commission, which sent him to France and Micheline several months of the year. The day after he retired, the general gave an interview explaining that it wasn't a soldier's aim to promote death, but to promote life:

> Let's not talk high-sounding phrases. Let's not use old words, shopworn words, words like "glory" and "peace" without thinking exactly what they mean. There's no "glory" in killing. There's no "glory" in maiming men. There are the glorious dead, but they would be more glorious living. The most glorious thing is life. And we who are alive must cling to it, each of us helping.[3]

His only continuing official responsibilities were with the Monuments Commission, though he remained active with other projects. In 1928 he hosted a fund-raising dinner for the National Cathedral in Washington, whose cornerstone had been laid by President Theodore Roosevelt in 1907, but which was still in the early stages of construction. In his remarks he made one of few lengthy comments on the record about his religious views.

> As a strong believer in adequate preparedness, it is my conviction that the real strength of the nation rests on the religious sentiment of the citizens. The capital of the nation is the strategic point at which to make a demonstration of our common Christianity.
>
> To try to build a worthy nation without God is impossible. I welcome you tonight, therefore, not only as friends, but as co-workers in an enterprise which seems to me of vital importance to the future of our country—the hastening of the day when it can no longer be said that [in] Washington, the capital of the United States, there is no adequate expression of the religious faith of the people.
>
> My chief interests are the building of monuments in France to the memory of the service of American soldiers in the War, and assisting to build this great cathedral to the glory of Him to Whom we owe all our greatness. Many cathedrals, unfortunately, have been destroyed in wars, and I, for one, should like to have a hand in building a cathedral.[4]

The cathedral was finished in 1990.

Ever the teacher, the general decided to use his unaccustomed free time to write his memoirs, sharing the lessons of his lifetime of experience and leaving what he considered an accurate historical record. He worked on the project in his opulent office at the War Department, which had been granted him for life. Visitors were always impressed with its high ceilings, two fireplaces, mahogany doors, parquet floors, and elegant fittings.

Pershing fretted over his writing, determined to include every fact, every person, and every military unit. He squeezed all the passion and excitement out of the story by obsessing over details. His accounts of battle scenes were especially dull. He had assistants pore over the prose, counting the number of mentions of each unit and commander, then went back and added more about those he felt he had slighted. George Marshall called the final product "too detailed for the general reader and not detailed enough for military students . . . a confused mass of little events"[5] that obscured the big picture.

Colonel Marshall also privately questioned Pershing about his decision to omit General Peyton March from his memoirs altogether. March was chief of staff at the end of the war. Pershing disliked him intensely because March criticized and opposed some of his organizational and command decisions about the AEF. Pershing thought March, back in Washington, had no grounds for second-guessing Pershing's orders in the field. Believing his role was unfairly downplayed in Pershing's account, General March wrote his own book criticizing Pershing for being insufficiently trained, too slow to engage the enemy, overspending on unnecessary equipment, and more. Then it was Pershing's turn to be furious. His friends persuaded him not to respond in public because it would only draw attention to the claims.

General Pershing spent years on his war memoir and claimed to hate the entire process. He thought his writing was flat and unexciting. He might well have given up the project if not for a sense of responsibility he felt to leave an accurate historical record and share whatever lessons he could. The final result, *My Experiences in the World War*, was published in 1931 in two volumes totaling 836 pages. Reviewers judged its author as one who had been cold, severe, and iron-fisted, but whose ultimate aim was to maintain the discipline required to win the war with the fewest casualties possible. For all its literary shortcomings, Pershing's effort was awarded the 1932 Pulitzer Prize for History.

During the period he labored over his manuscript, General Pershing's world gradually changed around him. In the spring of 1929, Pershing was in France when Marshal Ferdinand Foch died, and he attended his funeral at Les Invalides, the resting place of Napoleon. In November of the same year, Senator Warren died after thirty-seven years in office, longer than any U.S. senator in history. His funeral was held in the Senate chamber, with burial in Cheyenne next to the general's precious Frankie and their three daughters.

The senator's grandson and namesake, Warren Pershing, graduated from Yale in 1931 and joined a Wall Street broker-age firm. General Pershing cautioned his son against a career in finance with the world economy in decline, but Warren contin-ued with his career plan and soon prospered.

General Pershing was the nation's official host in 1931 when Marshal Pétain led a French delegation to the United States to mark the 150th anniversary of General Cornwallis's surrender at Yorktown, ending the American Revolutionary War. The two old friends were together constantly during the visit, recalling the war years and trading warm compliments. Pershing called his French counterpart "a master of the art of war, a leader who can inspire whole armies with his patriotism, determination, valor."[6]

Even as he remained involved in various projects, the general eased into a life of retirement. He moved during the years from a house in Chevy Chase, Maryland, to an apartment on Connecticut Avenue where Senator Warren had lived, to an elegant but smaller apartment in the Carlton Hotel. He spent relatively little time in Washington. Part of every year he took a vacation out west, and he still spent several months at a time in France. He went to see his sister May in Lincoln and to visit the Warren ranch in Wyoming. Pershing never learned to drive a car. When he didn't travel by train, he was content to have Warren chauffeur him in his regal Cadillac. The *Washington Post* named the general the best-dressed man in Washington, his civilian dress always as spotless and perfectly tailored as his uniforms.

General Douglas MacArthur became army chief of staff in 1930 and held the position for five years. He had not been Pershing's first choice for the job. Pershing thought MacArthur was too affected, too self-promoting, too much of a grandstander. However, he strongly endorsed MacArthur's efforts to keep Congress from continuing to cut money from American defense spending. As the worldwide economic depression deepened, Pershing and others saw signs of rearmament in Germany that American politicians seemed eager to ignore in their concentration on economic recovery.

One proposal was to reduce General Pershing's military pension. Pershing received $18,000 per year plus about $3,000 in allowances, making him the second-highest paid government employee in the country behind President Calvin Coolidge. MacArthur insisted that Pershing's salary be maintained, and in the end Congress backed down. This did not mean that Pershing was a rich man. His investment portfolio was in ruins like everyone else's. And he sent financial support to a number of relatives, friends, children of friends, and to Micheline.

In the spring of 1937, the year the general dedicated his last war monument at Ypres, President Franklin D. Roosevelt sent Pershing as his representative to the coronation of King George VI. Pershing joined the crush of seventy-seven hundred guests in Westminster Abbey on May 12, dressed for the occasion in ceremonial uniform with sword, sash, gold collar and cuffs, and ostrich feathered hat. He also attended the state banquet at Buckingham Place and the palace ball.

He was unexpectedly reminded of the experience later when he took an interest in broadcasting. On a whim he called a Washington radio station to ask if he could come watch a show being produced. The woman on the phone asked who was calling.

"General Pershing," the caller said.

"Really. Now isn't that nice! You come right down, General Pershing, and when you get here, ask for Queen Mary. That's who I am." (Mary was the new king's mother.)

In half an hour Pershing arrived at the radio station and asked for Queen Mary. When the woman came out expecting a prankster, she was awestruck to see the retired General of the Armies in her waiting room.

The general went west in early 1938 for his usual vacation, traveling with his sister May to Arizona. At seventy-seven he suffered more from his frequent colds and fever than in the past. In February he was sick with kidney and heart trouble that sent him to the hospital in serious condition. By the twenty-fourth, the wire services were reporting the ailing general was "dangerously near death."[7] One of his aides sent a telegram to Micheline in Paris. His former aide and strategist, now General George C. Marshall, hurried west. The army flew Pershing's dress uniform to Tucson for him to be buried in.

But against all odds, the general recovered. Though he was never strong again, he was well enough to attend Warren's wedding in New York on April 22, traveling by private railroad car from Tucson to a siding beneath the Waldorf-Astoria. The bride, Muriel Bache Richards, was the granddaughter of Jules S. Bache, a member of the J. P. Morgan firm and one of the most successful financiers in the country. Like the rest of the high society crowd at the ceremony, the general wore the traditional morning dress of cutaway coat and striped trousers. He was too weak to attend the reception, and returned to his hotel instead of the Bache mansion on Fifth Avenue, where guests celebrated surrounded by paintings by Rembrandt, Van Dyck, Titian, Raphael, Gainsborough, and Vermeer.

Pershing traveled to France for the last time in June 1939, returning to the United States on August 17. Two weeks later a revived and rearmed Germany invaded Poland and another world war began. To his old friend Charles Dawes, who had been vice president under Coolidge, he wrote that the idea was "a tragic thought for all of us who fought in the last World War and who believed that such a calamity could not again come upon the people."[8] By 1940 the Nazis had overrun all the ground Pershing and two million soldiers had reclaimed at such enormous cost. Again the French deserted and surrendered as this time the Germans marched triumphantly into Paris on June 14, gaining the prize Pershing had once denied them. The general's old friend and comrade Marshal Pétain agreed to head a puppet government under Hitler. Semi-senile at eighty-four, he was unwilling to subject his nation to another season of horrific bloodshed.

Pershing refused to believe Pétain would give up the fight, and he sent him a letter of encouragement. He also arranged to get Micheline out of Paris, sending her thousands of dollars and a letter to help her negotiate diplomatic channels. Warren met her at the pier in New York and settled her into an apartment at the Shoreham Hotel in Washington.

There were strong sentiments in Congress and in the public mind that America should not get involved in another foreign war. National military preparedness was still far below what Pershing thought it should be. The general asked for network radio time to address the American people on the issue. On August 4 he sat at a table in his apartment at the Carlton Hotel before a bank of microphones and newsreel cameras. Speaking slowly with perfect diction, his ever-raspy voice animated yet controlled, Pershing told America and the world that the United States had to prepare to fight again.

> We must be ready to meet force with a stronger force. We must build up our army and navy. We must have the strength of

character to face the truths. A new kind of war is loose in the world. It is a war against civilization, it is a revolution against the values which we have cherished. It must be faced with daring and devotion. We must lift up our hearts. We must reaffirm our noble traditions. We must make ourselves so strong that the tradition we live by shall not perish.

The Louisville *Courier-Journal* judged his speech "a noble call to truth-telling and to courage."[9]

In December 1940 President Roosevelt asked General Pershing to serve as America's ambassador to Vichy France, the German-controlled government headed by Pétain. The president hoped the old warrior could encourage his friend not to acquiesce to Nazi demands that the French go to war against Britain. Pershing declined the appointment, saying he was too old and infirm to carry out the duties. He was spending more time now at Walter Reed Army Hospital. His admirer and former aide, General George Marshall, now army chief of staff, personally drove around Washington to find a more suitable place for him to live than the Carlton. When no place was available, Pershing became a more or less permanent resident of Walter Reed, though he kept an apartment at the Carlton, as well as an office at the War Department.

One of his last public outings was to see the christening of his grandson, John Warren Pershing, born in January 1941. The June ceremony was moved from New York to Washington's National Cathedral so the general could attend. In July of that year, the film *Sergeant York* was released to rave reviews for both the story and its star, Gary Cooper. Pershing had given permission to be portrayed in the movie, even though the Hollywood version of history showed him awarding York the Medal of Honor, which had actually been presented by York's division commander. York and Pershing had met, however, when the general awarded him the Distinguished Service Medal.

After the attack on Pearl Harbor, Pershing wrote President Roosevelt offering his services "in any way in which my experience and strength, to the last ounce, will be of help in the fight."[10] The president replied immediately, declaring that the general was "magnificent" and that his services "will be of great value." While weakness kept the old general from even an advisory role, his son refused a commission from General Marshall and joined the army as a private. Warren fought in France and Germany, rising to the rank of major, then returned to his family and Wall Street after the war.

Pershing grew gradually weaker and less aware of the world around him. General Marshall came to visit as often as his duties would allow. The general's sister May moved from Nebraska into a guest house on the hospital grounds. Pershing and Charlie Dawes still met once a month for lunch. His old tank commander, General George Patton, came to call. The conflict over Patton's sister Nita was long in the past; she had never married. Patton knelt, kissed Pershing's hand, and asked for his blessing. The old man said, "Good-bye, Georgie. God bless you and keep you, and give you victory." Patton wrote Pershing regularly from the field. After his historic battles in the deserts of North Africa he declared, "I can assure you that whatever ability I have shown or shall show as a soldier is the result of a studious endeavor to copy the greatest American soldier, yourself."[11]

By the time the Germans surrendered on May 7, 1945, General Pershing was too weak to give the press the statement they requested. He was mentioned in the newspapers on September 13, his eighty-fifth birthday, when President Harry Truman sent birthday greetings. "This should be one of the happiest of your birthdays as you remember that this time we went all the way thru to Berlin as you counseled in 1918." Roosevelt had sent much the same greeting the year before: "None of us will forget that in 1918 you wanted to go through to Berlin. How right you were!"[12]

Pershing was saddened to hear that Marshal Pétain had been sentenced to death for treason after collaborating with the Germans. The sentence was commuted to life in prison, where the French leader died six years later at the age of ninety-five. News of Petain's fate was one of the few bits of information that registered with the general. Another was that when Douglas MacArthur came ashore in the Philippines after routing the Japanese, he was met by an old Moro warrior who said he was an ally of Pershing's and had been loyal to the United States ever since.

Aunt May and Micheline helped him pass the time reading, talking, and playing cards. Micheline, her beauty faded, her teeth so decayed that she covered them with a handkerchief when she laughed, remained devoted to the end. Warren's wife, Muriel or "Mumu," brought the grandsons to visit often—Pershing's second grandson, Richard, had been born in October 1942. Their presence and stories of their latest adventures always made him happy. He drifted in and out of sentience, sometimes alert and engaged, other times confused or silent. On July 15, 1948, John Joseph Pershing, General of the Armies, died in his sleep.

A day later, Warren, at his father's bequest, sent Micheline a large check and a letter the general had written in 1929 to be delivered at his death. He wrote that she was a gift to him from God and had made him happy. He hoped she wouldn't cry over him. A Catholic priest had secretly married them in Pershing's hospital room two years before Pershing's death. The general left a life insurance policy, issued in 1926, to Micheline and an estate of $250,000 in trust to May. Upon her death it would revert to Warren, himself a millionaire by virtue of his marriage and the success of his brokerage firm, Pershing & Co.

Pershing often said that he wanted to be buried with his men. Rather than joining Frankie and the girls in Cheyenne, he was interred at Arlington Cemetery with the same simple white marble headstone as every other soldier resting there. Three hundred thousand mourners lined the streets of Washington for his funeral on July 19. Leading a contingent of sixteen generals in the procession were Supreme Allied Commander Dwight D. Eisenhower and Army Chief of Staff Omar N. Bradley. As rain started to fall, Eisenhower asked Bradley if he thought they should get in a car.

"For Black Jack Pershing," Bradley replied, "I think it would be proper if we walked in the rain."[13]

Legacy

JOHN JOSEPH PERSHING was a teacher all his life. He attended West Point not because he was interested in the army but because it was free and he knew that in order to be a better teacher, he himself had to learn. He was a careful observer and keen analyzer who looked beneath the surface to see how the world worked. As a young officer in Cuba he saw the liabilities of ignoring lessons from the past. His superiors, who had never led men in battle, didn't learn how before they had to lead themselves. Until near the end of his life Pershing never stopped learning, never stopped teaching. He taught younger officers how to do their jobs. He taught the world how to grow old with a sense of honor and purpose. He taught two generations of soldiers that personal friendship must never get in the way of professional duty, and yet the responsibilities of command on the field need not separate friends anywhere else.

He also taught, by word and deed, men who literally rescued the world during and after World War II, the war Pershing warned would come as the result of an armistice and not a surrender in 1918. George C. Marshall, Pershing's chief of staff and a tactical mastermind, later rose to be a General of the Army, army chief of staff during World War II, and architect of the Marshall Plan that revived Europe after the war and allowed a defeated and devastated enemy the opportunity to recover. Japan developed the strongest per capita economy in Asia (currently four times higher than China), and Germany the largest and most important in Europe, because they were treated not as conquered foes but as fallen fellow human beings. Britain and France, the next-largest European economies, were also direct benefits of Marshall's genius, and indirectly of Pershing's legacy of fairness and honor.

Pershing saw the humanity in everyone. A reporter once said he could read a man's soul through his boots or his buttons. This was true whether the man was white, black, or any other color. In an era when racial discrimination was as prevalent and cruel as any time in history, Pershing as a teacher and leader was completely color-blind. His first job was teaching black children to read. His first military command was a cavalry unit of black soldiers. He committed himself fully to these responsibilities, treating his charges with respect, no differently than he would have treated any other race.

After the massacre at Wounded Knee, Pershing led a detail of Native American scouts at a time when they were despised as savages. As a commander in the Philippines, he treated the native Moros as equals, trusting them and earning their trust and pacifying them where others had failed. He dealt with the Mexicans, the French, and every other kind of people the same way: learning about them, understanding their needs, and then using that knowledge to achieve his objectives. He took on the responsibility of teaching them that, at their core, their needs and America's needs were the same: peace, freedom, respect, opportunity, and the pursuit of happiness.

For his extraordinary leadership abilities Pershing was appointed the first-ever General of the Armies. During the American Bicentennial celebration in 1976, President Gerald Ford raised George Washington to the same rank, preceding Pershing in seniority. There have been eight generals commissioned to the next-highest rank of General of the Army: U. S. Grant, William T. Sherman, Philip Sheridan, George Marshall, Douglas MacArthur, Dwight Eisenhower, Henry "Hap" Arnold, and Omar Bradley. There are no general officers at this five-star rank today.

The highest rank in the regular army is full general (four stars). There are currently forty-one active duty full generals in the U.S. military, including twelve in the army. These dozen officers, eleven men and a woman, lead a fighting force John J. Pershing could never have imagined, but which would not surprise him. Whatever his name recognition, General Pershing leaves a rich legacy deeply woven into the fabric of American military life and tradition. His strict observation of regulations, attention to detail, sense of humanity, purpose, patriotism, bravery, compassion, fairness, and self-sacrifice are the building blocks of today's military successes. Their absences are at the root of its failures.

More than sixty years after his death, Black Jack Pershing is still teaching. Remembered as a stern taskmaster, he was driven not by devotion to discipline but by devotion to duty. Not only was there honor and order in his methods, there also was victory. And that is the lesson this teacher leaves with us.

Notes

CHAPTER 1

1. Letter from Pershing to the class reunion of 1911, quoted in Smith, *Until the Last Trumpet Sounds*, 22.

2. Letter from Pershing to his classmates 1887, quoted in Smith, *Until the Last Trumpet Sounds*, 26.

3. Ibid.

CHAPTER 2

1. Letter from Pershing, away on patrol, to Penn, 10/10/1887, quoted in Smith, *Until the Last Trumpet Sounds*, 30.

2. Smith, *Until the Last Trumpet Sounds*, 32.

3. Letter from Pershing to Penn, 9/30/1890, quoted in Smythe, *Guerrilla Warrior: The Early Life of John J. Pershing*, 19.

4. *Aberdeen* [South Dakota] *Sunday Pioneer*, January 3, 1891.

5. Letter from Pershing to Penn, 2/14/1891, quoted in Smythe, *Guerrilla Warrior*, 21.

6. Smith, *Until the Last Trumpet Sounds*, 41.

7. Ibid.

8. Andrews, *My Friend and Classmate*, 46.

9. Smith, *Until the Last Trumpet Sounds*, 44.

CHAPTER 3

1. Smith, *Until the Last Trumpet Sounds*, 48.

2. From Pershing's unpublished memoirs in the Library of Congress (henceforth Pershing Memoirs).

3. Lacey, *Pershing: A Biography*, 26.

4. Ibid., 28.

5. Pershing Memoirs.

6. Lacey, *Pershing: A Biography*, 29.

7. Pershing Memoirs.

8. Smythe, *Guerrilla Warrior*, 52.

9. Vandiver, *Black Jack*, 216.

CHAPTER 4

1. Goldhurst, *Pipe Clay and Drill*, 105.

2. Lacey, *Pershing: A Biography*, 36.

3. Smith, *Until the Last Trumpet Sounds*, 60.

4. Pershing Memoirs.

5. Lacey, *Pershing: A Biography*, 38.

6. Smith, *Until the Last Trumpet Sounds, 61.*

7. Pershing Memoirs.

8. Smythe, *Guerrilla Warrior*, 94.

9. Smith, *Until the Last Trumpet Sounds*, 65.

10. Ibid., 67.

11. Ibid.

12. Lacey, *Pershing: A Biography*, 45.

13. Ibid., 47.

CHAPTER 5

1. Smythe, *Guerrilla Warrior*, 113.

2. Miss Warren's diary entries here and following quoted in Smith, *Until the Last Trumpet Sounds*, 78ff.

3. Smith, *Until the Last Trumpet Sounds*, 80.

4. Lacey, *Pershing: A Biography*, 51.

5. Ibid., 52.

6. Ibid., 53.

7. Smith, *Until the Last Trumpet Sounds*, 88.

8. Ibid., 91.

9. Smythe, *Guerrilla Warrior*, 126.

10. Lacey, *Pershing: A Biography*, 56.

11. Smith, *Until the Last Trumpet Sounds*, 97.

CHAPTER 6

1. Lacey, *Pershing: A Biography*, 58.

2. Letters between General and Mrs. Pershing here and following quoted in Smith, *Until the Last Trumpet Sounds*, 100ff.

3. Pershing Memoirs.

4. Lacey, *Pershing: A Biography*, 64.

5. Pershing Memoirs.

6. Letter from Pershing to Moro leaders, 12/6/1911.

7. Lacey, *Pershing: A Biography*, 72.

CHAPTER 7

1. Pershing Memoirs.

2. Smith, *Until the Last Trumpet Sounds*, 126.

3. Smythe, *Guerrilla Warrior*, 210.

4. Ibid., 208.

5. Smith, *Until the Last Trumpet Sounds*, 132.

6. Ibid.

7. Ibid., 136.

CHAPTER 8

1. Blumenson, *The Patton Papers*, 320. Quoted in multiple sources.

2. Smith, *Until the Last Trumpet Sounds*, 148.

3. Ibid., 149.

4, Ibid., 148.

5. Smythe, *General of the Armies*, 6.

6. Ibid., 17.

7. Goldhurst, *Pipe Clay and Drill*, 360.

8. Smith, *Until the Last Trumpet Sounds*, 155.

CHAPTER 9

1. Smythe, *General of the Armies*, 22.

2. Bullard, *Personalities and Reminiscences*, 94.

3. *Detroit Free Press*, February 5, 1922.

4. Lacey, *Pershing: A Biography*, 102.

5. *American Legion Monthly*, November 1928.

6. Smith, *Until the Last Trumpet Sounds*, 162.

7. Smythe, *General of the Armies*, 58.

8. Smith, *Until the Last Trumpet Sounds*, 166.

9. Smythe, *General of the Armies*, 43.

10. Smith, *Until the Last Trumpet Sounds*, 168.

CHAPTER 10

1. Smith, *Until the Last Trumpet Sounds*, 169.

2. Ibid., 173.

3. Ibid., 172.

4. Ibid., 177.

5. Smythe, *General of the Armies*, 26.

6. Pershing, *My Experiences in the World War*, vol. II, 305.

7. Ibid., 307.

8. Lacey, *Pershing: A Biography*, 135.

9. Pershing, *My Experiences in the World War*, 29.

10. Smith, *Until the Last Trumpet Sounds*, 181.

11. Smythe, *General of the Armies*, 135.

12. Smythe, *Guerrrilla Warrior*, 129.

CHAPTER 11

1. Smythe, *General of the Armies*, 132.

2. Lacey, *Pershing: A Biography*, 141.

3. Kozaryn, "Marines' First Crucible."

4. Smythe, *General of the Armies*, 169.

5. Smith, *Until the Last Trumpet Sounds*, 185.

6. Ibid., 186.

7. Lacey, *Pershing: A Biography*, 143–4.

8. Ibid., 146–7.

9. Smith, *Until the Last Trumpet Sounds*, 188.

10. Ibid., 189.

11. Lacey, *Pershing: A Biography*, 147.

12. Smith, *Until the Last Trumpet Sounds*, 189.

13. Lacey, *Pershing: A Biography*, 154.

14. Ibid., 155.

CHAPTER 12

1. Smythe, *General of the Armies*, 186.

2. Harbord, *American Army in France*, 433.

3. Smythe, *General of the Armies*, 191.

4. Ibid., 200.

5. Ibid.

6. Griscom, *Diplomatically Speaking*, 435.

7. Smith, *Until the Last Trumpet Sounds*, 193, 201.

8. Lacey, *Pershing: A Biography*, 170.

9. Ibid., 171.

10. Smith, *Until the Last Trumpet Sounds*, 200.

11. Ibid.

12. Smythe, *General of the Armies*, 237.

CHAPTER 13

1. Smith, *Until the Last Trumpet Sounds*, 219.

2. Ibid., 200.

3. Letters between Pershing and Micheline Resco here and following quoted in Smith, *Until the Last Trumpet Sounds*, 221ff.

4. Smith, *Until the Last Trumpet Sounds*, 222.

5. Ibid., 224.

6. Ibid.

7. Ibid., 225.

8. Ibid., 226

9. Ibid.

10. Ibid., 231.

11. Ibid., 233.

12. Ibid., 235.

13. Ibid., 237.

14. Lacey, *Pershing: A Biography*, 180.

CHAPTER 14

1. "Pershing Denies 'Exile' Order Rumor," *New York Times*, February 10, 1922.

2. Lacey, *Pershing: A Biography*, 183.

3. Smith, *Until the Last Trumpet Sounds*, 257.

4. "Religion: Cathedral & Church," *Time*, March 5, 1928.

5. Smythe, *General of the Armies*, 292.

6. Smith, *Until the Last Trumpet Sounds*, 264.

7. Ibid., 277.

8. [For some reason I can't find this quote again. Will keep looking.]

9. Ibid., 285.

10. Ibid., 290.

11. Ibid., 294.

12. Ibid., 295.

13. Ibid., 314.

Bibliography

_____. *Aberdeen* [South Dakota] *Sunday Pioneer*, January 3, 1891.

_____. *American Legion Monthly*, November 1928.

Andrews, Avery DeLano. *My Friend and Classmate John J. Pershing*. Harrisburg: Military Service Publishing, 1939.

Blumenson, Martin. *The Patton Papers*. Boston: Houghton Mifflin, 1972–74.

Bullard, Robert Lee. *Personalities and Reminiscences of the War*. Garden City: Doubleday, Page, 1925.

Cooke, James J. *Pershing and His Generals: Command and Staff in the AEF*. Westport: Praeger, 1997.

_____. *Detroit Free Press*. February 5, 1922.

Goldhurst, Richard. *Pipe Clay and Drill*. New York: Reader's Digest Press, 1977.

Griscom, Lloyd. *Diplomatically Speaking*. Boston: Little, Brown, 1940.

Harbord, James G. *The American Army in France*. Boston: Little, Brown, 1936.

Kozaryn, Linda. "Marines' First Crucible: Belleau Wood." Armed Forces Press Service, 18 June 1998.

Lacey, Jim. *Pershing: A Biography*. New York: Palgrave Macmillan, 2008.

_____. "Pershing Denies 'Exile' Order Rumor." *New York Times*, February 10, 1922.

Pershing, John. *My Experiences in the World War*. New York: Frederick A. Stokes Company, 1931.

Pershing, John. Unpublished memoir. Library of Congress.

"Religion: Cathedral & Church." *Time*, March 5, 1928.

Smith, Gene. *Until the Last Trumpet Sounds: The Life of General of the Armies John J. Pershing*. New York: John Wiley & Sons, Inc. 1998.

Smythe, Donald. *Pershing: General of the Armies*. Bloomington: Indiana University Press, 1986.

_____. *Guerrilla Warrior: The Early Life of John J. Pershing*. New York: Charles Scribner's Sons, 1973.

Vandiver, Frank E. *Illustrious Americans: John J. Pershing*. Morristown: Silver Burdett. 1967.

_____. *Black Jack*. College Station: Texas A&M University Press, 1977.

Acknowledgments

WHEN STEPHEN MANSFIELD offered me the opportunity to contribute a volume on Black Jack Pershing to his excellent series on generals, I thought the nickname came from the nightstick policemen used to carry. The more I looked, the more surprised I was at how remarkable a man Pershing was and how tragically little I knew about him. Thank you, Stephen, for this project and the insights it has brought me about a great American leader. I'm hopeful the result will introduce him to others who will be as happy for his acquaintance as I have been.

Thanks also to my friends and colleagues at Thomas Nelson: Joel Miller, Kristen Parrish, Heather Skelton, and Lisa Schmidt. In a hundred different ways, they have made this book better and my time writing it more enjoyable. Janene MacIvor made a valuable contribution as copy editor.

I appreciate as always the patience and support of my children, Charles and Olivia, who now know more about Black Jack Pershing than they ever dreamed possible; and of my faithful friends Robert Thomison, Phillip Nappi, Ed Freeman, Tom Goddard, and David Beavers, ever ready with food and drink and conversation as the story unfolded. And special thanks to Pat Perry, who cracked the whip and cheered me on all the way from Paris.

I'm grateful to my agent, Andrew Wolgemuth, for good work and wise counsel that never fail, and to Robert Wolgemuth, for challenging us all to set ever higher standards, and to remember that everything we do is to the glory of God.

About the Author

JOHN PERRY WAS born in Kentucky and grew up in Houston. After serving in the U. S. Army infantry, he graduated from Vanderbilt University *cum laude*. He also studied at University College, Oxford, England.

John began his career as an advertising copywriter in Houston, moving to Nashville in 1983. John was a founder of Wolf, Perry & Clark Music and also of American Network Radio, where he produced and syndicated radio specials for Garth Brooks, Dolly Parton, and other country stars. His work for a chain of bookstores led to a marketing assignment for a publishing firm, which in turn led to John's transition from copywriter to author.

John is the biographer of Sergeant Alvin York and a Gold Medallion finalist for *Unshakable Faith*, a dual biography of

Booker T. Washington and George Washington Carver. For The Generals series he has previously written *Lee: A Life of Virtue*. He also is the author of *Lady of Arlington*, the biography of Mary Custis Lee, wife of Robert E. Lee, which was nominated for the Lincoln Prize for books on the Civil War era. His novel *Letters to God* was a *New York Times* best seller.

John lives in Belle Meade, former site of an antebellum plantation and thoroughbred farm near Nashville.